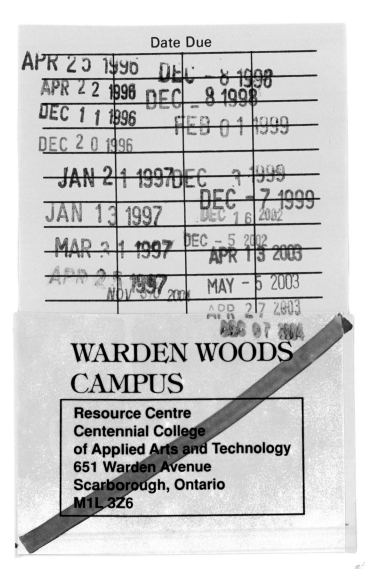

Canadian Fiction Studies

Other volumes in preparation

Introducing
MARGARET LAURENCE'S

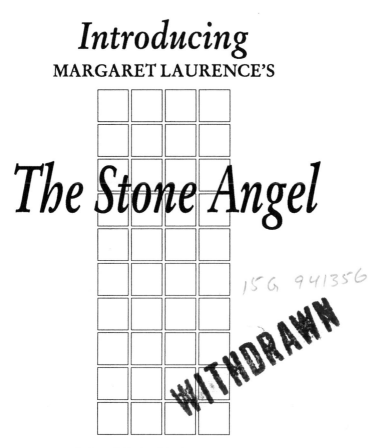

The Stone Angel

A READER'S GUIDE BY
George Woodcock

E C W P R E S S

CANADIAN CATALOGUING IN PUBLICATION DATA

Woodcock, George, 1912–
Introducing Margaret Laurence's The stone angel

(Canadian fiction studies ; no. 1)
Bibliography: p. 73
Includes index.
ISBN 1–55022–017–9

1. Laurence, Margaret, 1926–1986. The stone angel.
I. Title. II. Series.

PS8523.A86S763 1988   C813'.54   C88–095234–2
PR9199.3.L39S763 1989

This book has been published with the assistance of grants
provided by the Ontario Arts Council and The Canada Council.

The cover features a reproduction of the dust-wrapper from
the first edition of *The Stone Angel*, courtesy of the
Thomas Fisher Rare Book Library, University of Toronto.
Frontispiece photograph by D.W. Boult, Boult Photographics,
reproduced courtesy of David Laurence.

Design & imaging by ECW Production Services,
Sydenham, Ontario. Printed in Canada.

Distributed by University of Toronto Press
5201 Dufferin Street, North York, Ontario M3H 5T8

Published by ECW PRESS
307 Coxwell Avenue, Toronto, Ontario M4L 3B5

Table of Contents

A Note on the Author

Born in Winnipeg, George Woodcock went to England in his infancy, and remained there until 1949 when he returned to Canada, on whose Pacific coast he has lived ever since. While in England he founded *Now*, a radical literary magazine, which he ran from 1940 to 1947; acted for a period as editor of another journal, *Freedom*; and began to establish himself in the English literary world with his books of poetry, and prose works like *William Godwin: A Biography* (1946), and *The Paradox of Oscar Wilde* (1950). Since returning to Canada he has travelled in Asia, the Americas, the South Pacific, and Europe, and has produced many travel books. Some of these are *Incas and Other Men: Travels in the Andes* (1959), *Faces of India: A Travel Narrative* (1964), and *South Sea Journey* (1976). Most recently he has been to northwestern China, where he travelled up the Silk Road and into the Gobi Desert. He has also published more verse; a number of important critical works including *The Crystal Spirit: A Study of George Orwell* (1966), *Dawn and the Darkest Hour: A Study of Aldous Huxley* (1972), and *Thomas Merton: Monk and Poet* (1978); and a number of historical works including *The British in the Far East* (1969) and *Who Killed the British Empire: An Inquest* (1974).

His writing on Canada has been considerable. He founded the critical journal *Canadian Literature*; has written a history of the Doukhobors and a biography of Gabriel Dumont; and is the author of critical studies of Hugh MacLennan, Mordecai Richler, Matt Cohen, and Patrick Lane. Three volumes of his critical essays have been published: *Odysseus Ever Returning: Essays on Canadian Writers and Writings* (1970), *The World of Canadian Writing: Critiques and Recollections* (1980), and *Northern Spring: The Flowering of Canadian Literature* (1987). The first volume of his autobiography, *Letter to the Past*, appeared in 1982; the second volume, *Beyond the Blue Mountain*, appeared in 1987.

Introducing
Margaret Laurence's
The Stone Angel

Chronology

1926	Jean Margaret Wemyss born 16 July in Neepawa.
1944–47	Attends United College, Winnipeg. Completes B.A. in Honours English.
1947	Works as a reporter on the *Winnipeg Citizen*. Marries Jack Laurence, a hydraulic engineer.
1949	Moves to England.
1950	Moves to Somaliland, where Jack builds dams in the desert.
1952	Moves from Somaliland to Ghana. Jocelyn born.
1954	*A Tree for Poverty*. David born.
1957	Moves from Ghana to Vancouver.
1960	*This Side Jordan*.
1962	Separates from Jack Laurence. Moves with children to Buckinghamshire, England.
1963	*The Tomorrow-Tamer, The Prophet's Camel Bell*.
1964	*The Stone Angel*.
1966	*A Jest of God*.
1968	*Long Drums and Cannons: Nigerian Dramatists and Novelists 1952–1966*.
1969	Divorced from Jack Laurence.
1969	*The Fire-Dwellers*.
1970	*A Bird in the House, Jason's Quest*.
1971	Companion of the Order of Canada.
1974	Returns to Canada and lives henceforward at Lakefield, Ontario. *The Diviners*.
1975	Receives the Molson Award.
1976	*Heart of a Stranger*.
1979	*Six Darn Cows, The Olden Days Coat*.

1981	Appointed chancellor of Trent University.
	A Christmas Birthday Story.
1987	Died 5 January in Lakefield, Ontario.

Laurence's Life and Work

Few writers avoid writing about themselves, and Margaret Laurence was no exception. She admitted that at least one of her works of fiction was semiautobiographical. *A Bird in the House* (1970) is a series of stories, a kind of loosely connected novel, about a girl growing up in the small Manitoba town of Manawaka. The details, including the name of the town, are changed in many ways, but the stories essentially reproduce the pattern of their author's childhood development.

The young girl we see in *A Bird in the House*, Vanessa McLeod, grows up in a Presbyterian household in a prairie community and later escapes with relief into the wide world. She shares what we know were the ambitions of Margaret Wemyss. Like Vanessa Mc-Leod, Margaret Wemyss determined early on that she would be a writer, and she started by contributing stories to school magazines, and later to university magazines while she was at United College in Winnipeg. At the age of thirteen she sent a story to a *Winnipeg Free Press* competition, and in it, more than twenty years before she published *The Stone Angel*, she first used the name of Manawaka for a small fictional prairie town that resembled her native Neepawa. After graduating with a B.A. in Honours English in 1947, Margaret Wemyss began working on the *Winnipeg Citizen*. Shortly afterwards she married Jack Laurence, an engineer, and went with him to England. In 1950 Jack accepted the first of a series of engineering assignments that would keep the Laurences in Africa for seven years.

Margaret Laurence never wrote a novel about the first two years of her African life, which were spent in Somaliland, but the book she wrote about her experiences there — *The Prophet's Camel Bell* (1963) — not only describes vividly the life of the desert nomads she encountered while Jack Laurence was building ballehs, or earth dams, intended to conserve the rains that capriciously visited the desert and flowed away into the thirsty sands. It also offers a penetrating self-analysis of a young Canadian woman with vaguely liberal pretensions, who finds herself in a harsh desert land where the people survive — when they do survive — through pride and faith.

It was characteristic of Margaret Laurence, who declared that character was the all-important element in her novels, to remark, of leaving for Somaliland:

> And in your excitement at the trip, the last thing in the world that would occur to you is that the strangest glimpses you may have of any creature in the distant lands will be those you catch of yourself. (*The Prophet's* 1)

No one knows exactly how memories stored in the unconscious feed the imagination when a writer sets about writing fiction. But it is obvious that experiences which help reveal and liberate the inner self are important in the development of any novelist, and it is reasonable to conjecture that what happened to Laurence in Somaliland freed her mind from many of the comfortable assumptions about life acquired in a prairie small-town upbringing. By forcing her to see people who always lived in the shadow of death by starvation and thirst, it also projected her into the kind of existential crisis (or culture shock) which she would eventually resolve through creation.

Certainly in her next African home, where she lived for five years after leaving Somaliland, the process of creation started up, and Margaret Laurence began to develop into a mature writer. The country was the British West African colony of Gold Coast, then going through the period of rapid transition that led to its gaining independence as Ghana in 1957, the year the Laurences left. During the years preceding independence the British were preparing to leave, and many of them were already being set adrift by the Africanization of business and public services. The Africans themselves were joyful at the thought of liberation, and yet were often torn between loyalty to the tribal past, and the appeal of alien religions and lifestyles which they thought would enable them to enter the modern world as equals.

11

It was out of these conflicts and adaptations, and the small tragedies which they often precipitated, that Laurence, while she was still in Africa, began writing her first works of fiction, *This Side Jordan* (1960), a novel, and *The Tomorrow-Tamer* (1963), a volume of short stories. Laurence afterwards said that her period in Africa had a crucial influence on the way she developed as a writer.

I was fortunate in going to Africa when I did — in my early twenties — because for some years I was so fascinated by the African scene that I was prevented from writing an autobiographical first novel. I don't say there is anything wrong in autobiographical novels, but it would not have been the right thing for me — my view of the prairie town from which I had come was still too prejudiced and distorted by closeness. (*Heart* 14)

The distant, rather than the close view has always been important for Laurence, and it was in Vancouver, after her return to Canada, that she found the proper forms and tones for her books about Africa and began to publish her stories in literary magazines. In this way she established a pattern of writing while away from the settings of her books.

After she had finished writing about Africa in Vancouver, she went to live in England in 1962. It was there that she began to write Canadian books, the group of five great works of fiction centred on the prairies (though not exclusively about them), that began with *The Stone Angel* (1964). *The Stone Angel* established Margaret Laurence as a leading Canadian novelist, and not only in Canada. It was well received in England, and the New York publisher Knopf launched her American career in a dramatic way by publishing three of her books — *New Wind in a Dry Land* (their title for *The Prophet's Camel Bell*), *The Tomorrow-Tamer*, and *The Stone Angel* — on the same day in 1964.

The Stone Angel was followed by *A Jest of God* (1966), *The Fire-Dwellers* (1969), *A Bird in the House* (1970), and *The Diviners* (1974). It was not a series like *The Forsyte Saga* or the Jalna novels in the sense of the same individual or family taking central place in each novel. But the novels, with their separate heroines, were nevertheless linked by a single community, and sometimes by the movement of a major character in one novel óver the stage to become a minor character in another. Laurence never lived in the prairies while writing of them, for when she did go back to Canada in 1974 she settled in Lakefield (where Catharine Parr Traill had once lived), and wrote the last of her Canadian novels, *The Diviners*, largely in her summer cottage on the Otonabee River near Peterborough.

But in her imagination she constantly returned to the plains of her childhood and to the fictional town of Manawaka from where the central characters of all her novels set off, even if they eventually live and — in the case of the heroine in *The Stone Angel* — die away from home. This, she recognized, was her true "place to stand on," even though as a writer she needed to distance herself from it to gain the right objectivity with which to write of the land and the loneliness and isolation that she remembered from childhood. As she remarked:

I doubt if I will ever live there again, but those poplar bluffs and the blackness of that soil and the way in which the sky is open from one side of the horizon to the other — these are things I will carry inside my skull for as long as I live, with the vividness of recall that only our first home can have for us. (*Heart* 16)

In addition to the vividly portrayed Canadian setting (whether of the prairies or the Pacific coast), another important feature distinguished all the Manawaka novels from her African fiction. In *This Side Jordan* the main protagonists, the white Johnnie Kestoe and the black Nathaniel Amegbe, were both male, and so were the leading characters of the many stories in *The Tomorrow-Tamer*. In *The Prophet's Camel Bell*, it is mostly men that Laurence so sympathetically describes, because in the male-dominated society of Somaliland, it was mostly men that she encountered. She was seeking, as a stranger, to empathize with unfamiliar cultures and their social attitudes. But back in Canada she returned to her own world of experience, and from this time onward women were the central figures in her fiction, and through their eyes the world was seen. Margaret Laurence was a feminist, concerned that women should live equally with men, but she was not a narrow or dogmatic one — the men in her novels are depicted with sympathy and understanding, and often play crucial roles assisting the women in their search for self-knowledge. Her novels are not women's literature in the narrow, exclusive sense. They are universal in their appeal; whatever our gender, we enter freely into the minds and feelings of her characters, and always emerge a little wiser from the experience. Laurence's writing was not confined to her novels and short stories. Her first book, *A Tree for Poverty: Somali Poetry and Prose* (1954), was an essay on Somali oral and written literature accompanied by translations of stories and poems; it was the only work she actually wrote during her two years in Somaliland. Later on, memories of years in Ghana helped her to write *Long Drums and Cannons*, a critical study of Nigerian novelists and dramatists writing in English. She wrote some essays for magazines, which she eventually collected in *Heart of a Stranger*, in which she tells of her travels and also includes some very illuminating essays about her own work.

After she had completed *The Diviners*, Laurence said that she would write no more novels about Manawaka. In fact, in the last twelve years of her life she wrote no novels at all. But those final years, before she died of cancer in 1987, were by no means silent. While writing her novels she also wrote a children's book as a relaxation, *Jason's Quest* (1970), later followed by three more: *Six Darn Cows* (1979), *The Olden Days Coat* (1979) and *The Christmas Birthday Story* (1980). She was active in many other ways. She served as chancellor of Trent University and she became deeply involved in the nuclear disarmament movement. One of her most impressive pieces of writing in her last years was the convocation address she gave in 1982 at Emmanuel College, University of Victoria, in which she declared her faith in faith and, reaching back into the Christian background which she had never wholly abandoned, ended with a declaration as biblical as anything in her novels:

> If we have been given any commandment, as I believe we have, then surely it must mean that we pray and work and speak out for peace, and for human and caring justice for all people that on earth do dwell. ("A Statement" 60)

It will not escape the careful reader of *The Stone Angel* that the final phrase of that address, "all people that on earth do dwell," also appears at a crucial point in the novel (291), heralding Hagar Shipley's coming to terms as best she can with her life and her world.

In her last months Margaret Laurence was clearly coming to terms with her own life, for she spent them largely on writing an autobiography that was incomplete when she died.

The Importance of the Work

At the time of their writing, books can achieve importance for one or both of two reasons. They can be significant for their role in the development of a culture, which means that they have to be considered within their historical context. And they can be valued for their intrinsic qualities, the qualities that make them stand as works in their own right.

In the long run, the latter is the more important. Many books that seem very topical when they are published, lose their meaning as literary fashions or moral attitudes change, and remain interesting only to the social or cultural historian. The books that have lasting intrinsic value are those written with such imaginative intensity and formal skill that they can still appeal to our minds and stir our feelings even after the age to which they belong has slipped away into history. They survive because each creates a world for itself to live in, and so becomes impervious to the passing of time. We still sail through the seas with Odysseus and share his predicaments as if he were a contemporary adventurer, although his world lies buried under the detritus of almost three thousand years. Don Quixote still clatters on an immortal swaybacked Rosinante through our imaginations, as tenaciously alive as on the day his sorrowful countenance first began to haunt the thoughts of Miguel de Cervantes in the seventeenth century. And the company of fascinating characters with whom Tolstoy peopled *War and Peace* remain as alive as ever in the minds of modern man, though the real armies of 1812 have long marched away into the depersonalizing shadows of history. I cannot imagine a time when the *Odyssey, Don Quixote*, and *War and Peace* will cease to be read.

The Stone Angel, I suggest, is important for both the reasons I have listed. First, it came at a crucial stage in the development of Canadian

15

fiction, which was moving forward from its formative stages. It was moving away from the stylistic clumsiness of writers like Frederick Philip Grove, who sought to see prairie life in terms of an outdated European naturalism, and from the didactic earnestness of writers like Hugh MacLennan, who, in heavily thematic novels like *Barometer Rising* and *Two Solitudes*, had given us fictional lessons in the rise of a Canadian national consciousness and in the perils to national unity presented by the existence of French and English cultures living beside each other in mutual isolation.

Balancing literary accounts in the second edition of the *Literary History of Canada* (1976), Claude Bissell refers to Margaret Laurence as the "major novelist of the sixties" (9), a position she began to move into in the minds of critics and readers from the time *The Stone Angel* appeared. In the same history, W.H. New remarks that while the fifties had been MacLennan's decade, the sixties "was the decade of [Malcolm] Lowry (paradoxically, for he died in 1957) and of Margaret Laurence" (234). Bissell asserts that although Laurence "went back again and again to her prairie roots, [she] had no overt interest in national problems" (9), and New tells us that Laurence "explored the essential differences between middle-class expectations and other values, articulated a female perspective, and offered evidence to many younger writers to affirm that the simple fact of being alive was a political act" (234).

Both critics are right. Laurence came at a time when MacLennan's didacticism had served its purpose; what we needed now were not so much arguments to convince us, as myths to sustain our convictions. In creating and peopling her fictional town of Manawaka, Margaret Laurence offered a powerful myth of our country as it could exist, not in the statistics of the scientific historians, but in the imaginations of artists and their responsive audiences. Laurence's role as a woman novelist at that time was crucial. She built on the pioneering achievements of earlier writers like Sara Jeannette Duncan and Ethel Wilson, shifting the literary point of view in Canada away from being a dominantly male one, and since *The Stone Angel* was published, the activity and the importance of women writers has steadily increased in Canada.

Finally, there are the changes in attitude to form that began to appear in Canadian fiction during the 1960s, which are at least partly attributable to Margaret Laurence's influence. By establishing two parallel but different time systems in *The Stone Angel,* she contributed to the abandonment of the chronologically linear pattern traditionally associated with realist fiction; in her later novels she experimented even more radically with time and memory. *The Stone Angel* was also influential because, while earlier Canadian novelists had regarded the theme of a work of fiction as primary, and worked outward from it (as Hugh MacLennan did in all his novels), Margaret Laurence abandoned this intellectually oriented approach, proceeding in a more organic way through the imaginative creation of a character out of which the theme would naturally emerge rather than being imposed. In this sense, Margaret Laurence as a creative writer was ahead of the fashionable critical trend of the 1960s, which, following the pronouncements of Northrop Frye, tended to be based on the identification of themes. There is a touch of irony in the fact that the theme of survival which Laurence herself recognized as emerging naturally from *The Stone Angel* became the dominating idea and provided the title for one of the leading works of thematic criticism during that period — Margaret Atwood's *Survival.*

Thus for many reasons *The Stone Angel* stands as an influential book in the development of a true Canadian literature during the 1960s and subsequent decades, and will continue to interest future cultural historians. It is also likely to interest social historians for the way it portrays several generations of farming life on the prairie, and middle-class life on the Pacific coast, and perhaps especially for the way Laurence uses her characters' speech patterns as indicators of class and generation.

But the final test of a work of literature is whether it retains the interest of readers who are not literary or historical specialists. We talk of writers surviving, of books continuing to live, and by this we mean that they find readers, generation after generation, who feel that they are entering not only the minds of the characters but also the fictional world they inhabit. Critics and literary historians have often argued about the reasons why some books continue to be read a hundred years after they were written, and others, popular at the time of publication, are quickly forgotten. I suggest that the secret lies in a combination of universality and uniqueness. The characters must be presented, through their thoughts, action, and speech, in such a way that readers from other cultures can continue to identify with them. But no character can exist in a timeless vacuum. The environment, the fictional world that the novelist creates for them to live in, must be unique and self-consistent, so that it continues to exist in a kind of time capsule that inhabitants of other ages and places can enter through their identification with the characters. I believe *The Stone Angel* will survive because it fulfils both these requirements. Hagar Shipley, its heroine, is a universal personification of the urge to survive, and it is no accident that, as Laurence once remarked, North American readers accepted her as everybody's grandmother. Yet at the same time she is fiercely independent as a character in her own right, a whole personality. In the same way, by creating her fictional town of Manawaka, Margaret Laurence has on one level epitomized the characteristics of all small prairie towns; indeed, of all rural towns everywhere. Yet Manawaka as we experience it in *The Stone Angel* is unique, a self-contained world of the imagination that will survive in the mind long after the actual prairie communities of which it reminds one have passed away.

Critical Reception

One of the problems involved in considering a work of literature, whether a novel or a poem, is the importance we must attach to the author's declared intentions. It has often been argued, especially by the New Critics who dominated American literary scholarship for several decades, that it is a fallacy even to consider such intentions, since once a work of art is produced, it attains a kind of objective autonomy, and exists independently of the writer or his or her declared intention. I would argue that this attitude cuts us off from an understanding of the process of creation, and without that understanding — which involves a knowledge of the writer's intentions and the way he or she sets about implementing them — we cannot have a full understanding of the work.

On the other hand, a critical approach based entirely on a knowledge of the writer's intentions and his or her methods would also give us an incomplete understanding of the work, since even in the process of creation, the unconscious as well as the conscious mind is at work. The great psychoanalyst Carl Gustav Jung made the very important suggestion that one's unconscious, out of which the creative urge emerges, really has two dimensions: a personal one that contains the forgotten or repressed content of the individual's mental life, and a collective one which includes mental patterns shared with people of the same culture or even of the whole human race. These mental patterns create archetypes, universal images and symbols that recur in dreams and mythology and art, and often astonish us into recognizing how close we are in our imaginative lives to people who live in entirely different times and places.

This means that while the writer may knowingly control the conscious planning and creation of his or her work, elements may enter from the unconscious that he or she does not immediately recognize. I can quote one example that relates directly to Laurence,

19

one that involves a relationship between her perceptions as creator and my perceptions as a critic of her work. About ten years ago David Helwig was putting together a book of critical essays and he invited me to write a piece on Laurence. By that time a great deal of criticism had already been written of her individual books, but it seemed to me that nobody had yet found a convincing pattern of archetypes that united the four major novels of the Manawaka cycle. Then, reading *The Stone Angel* again, I recognized that what characterized Hagar Shipley more than anything else was her choleric temperament. This took me back to the old idea of the four humours regarded in the middle ages as dominating human physiology and human temperament. People were regarded as falling into four basic categories related to the four elements, of which, according to philosophers as early as Empedocles in the fifth century, the universe was composed: earth, air, fire, and water. The humour corresponding to earth is the choleric; to air, the phlegmatic; to fire, the sanguine; and to water, the melancholic.

Being impressed with how clearly all Hagar Shipley's actions and reactions fit in with what we think of as a choleric temperament, I went back to the novel and could not fail to notice the attachment Hagar showed to earth. Her memories are filled with highly concrete and detailed descriptions of natural scenes and their natural beauty, while the novel as a whole is instinct with the most sensual awareness of the earth's surface, of its creatures (animal or vegetable), of its colours and textures and smells. Hagar is an intensely visual but even more an intensely tactile person, concerned with what is evident to the sense of feeling, whether it is sex remembered vividly and in detail half a life afterwards, or the texture of a dress she wears in old age. Even her own body she often apprehends in terms of earthly mass, the way sculptors seem to apprehend the forms within the mineral masses with which they work. (And of course a sculptor's work — stone from the earth — gives the novel its title and beginning.) Even as she approaches death and her life is dominated more and more by the immaterial world of memory, the memories themselves tend to be defined and initiated by the material objects from the past which surround her and which she treasures.

Having noted how well Hagar and her temperament fitted in with the archetype of the element earth, I turned to the three other major works of the Manawaka cycle. *The Fire-Dwellers*, I was immediately aware, perfectly fitted the pattern; from its title and its double epigraphs relating to fire, it is haunted by a vision of conflagration, of a world threatened by conflagration due to human folly; while the mind of the central character, Stacey MacAindra, is an inferno of unfulfilled desires, fed by the fires of a sanguine and insatiable temperament. *A Jest of God* starts off with the children's rhyme, "The wind blows low, the wind blows high." Wind is air, and air is the element of Rachel Cameron; air that is insubstantial and wavering, that flees from fire and yet feeds it, as in the incident of the pentecostal meeting at which Rachel is unwillingly touched by the flames of inspiration and realizes to her horror that she has been speaking in tongues before strangers. Rachel's humour fits in with her element, for she is essentially phlegmatic; apathy as well as timidity prevent her from making decisions until they are forced on her. When she leaves for her new home in Vancouver (a change of air, as it were), it is air that seems to convey her, and she has an image of the bus carrying her away from Manawaka — not as an earth-borne vehicle, but as one that "flies along, smooth and confident as a great owl through the darkness" (201). Air is her element and in the end her liberation. Finally, *The Diviners* is associated by its very title with water, one of its leading characters is a water diviner, and the novel opens with the famous image of a river that seems to move both ways and is intimately related to the inner life of Morag, the leading character. Morag, typically for those associated with the element of water, is melancholic in temperament. Furthermore, she is a writer, and from the days when ancient poets drank of Apollo's spring at Delphi down to Shelley's death by drowning and Keats's description of himself as "one whose name was writ in water," water has been associated with poetry and by extension with writing in general.

I developed these insights in an essay called "The Human Elements: Margaret Laurence's Fiction," which eventually formed part of my book *The World of Canadian Writing* (1980). When Laurence heard of the radio talk in which I had tried out my ideas before the essay was published, she was greatly interested and I sent her a copy. When she read my script she rang me up and admitted that all the evidence I had given was there in her novels, and that the linking of her own symbolism with archetypes of the four elements now seemed so obvious that she was surprised nobody had noticed it before. But she had not deliberately set out to pattern her novels on the elements or the humours, and she thought that this was an excellent example of the way in which archetypal elements could enter into literature without the writer being aware of it. It was also, she thought, an example of the way critics sometimes help writers to a fuller understanding of the dimensions of their work.

I have told this tale of the relationship between a writer and a critic because it demonstrates the limitations of an interpretation of a work of literature that is based solely on a knowledge of the intention of a writer or of the way she wrote her book. But it would be equally limiting to ignore such matters, particularly in the case of writers who have gone to some pains to explain their attitudes toward the art of fiction and how their novels have taken shape in the processes of conception and completion.

Margaret Laurence in fact wrote two kinds of essays about her work and its background. Some of these are important in helping us to define the content of her work and the background to her life, which to her are obviously as closely linked as they are in the minds of her readers. "A Place to Stand On" discusses the reality of remembered experience behind her fictional community of Manawaka. "The Shack" describes the little home beside the Otonabee where she wrote *The Diviners*, and offers some clues about how the life she was living at the time entered into the book. "Where the World Began" discusses the matter of ancestry, a concern in all of Laurence's fiction. It reaches the conclusion, which her novels exemplify, that real ancestry does not mean the long line of forefathers a person may claim in other lands; it means the past of the world where you were born and grew up, and where the ancestors are "both my own and other people's ancestors who become mine" (*Heart* 219). Another essay, "Man of Our People," is about the great Métis leader Gabriel Dumont, whom Laurence admired. For her he is as much an ancestor as her own forebears who immigrated from the Scottish highlands: "his life, his legend, and his times are a part of our past which we desperately need to understand and pay heed to" (*Heart* 212).

These were the pieces that Margaret Laurence chose to include in her rather personal book of essays, *Heart of a Stranger*. But there are three other important essays which she did not include. They have a different and more serious tone, partly because they are addressed to people closely interested in literature, and partly because they very directly concern writing and her ideas about it. One of these was "Ten Years' Sentences," which I published in the tenth-anniversary issue of *Canadian Literature* (1969); another, "Time and the Narrative Voice," was written for John Metcalf's anthology, *The Narrative Voice* (1972), and the third, "Gadgetry or Growing: Form and Voice in the Novel," given as a talk when she was writer-in-residence at Toronto in 1970, was published in the *Journal of Canadian Fiction* in 1980. Taken together, these essays, which cover aspects of fiction such as character and fictional time, and the relationship between form and voice in fiction, give one a good idea of how Laurence saw the art of the novel, and how she used her insights in practice. I shall return to them in the next chapter when I consider the text itself: I think her ideas can best be discussed against the background of her actual work.

Actual criticism of Laurence's work began slowly but took on impetus after the publication of *The Stone Angel* in 1964. As early as 1955 her college friend Adele Wiseman reviewed *A Tree for Poverty* in *Queen's Quarterly*, and her African fiction received short and usually rather unimportant notices as it appeared, although Mary Renault wrote a bright review of *This Side Jordan* in which she remarked that Laurence "has an impressive sense of the equatorial rhythms: the cruelty, the gay or the wistful resignation, the feckless humour, the splendid hymns" (124). Henry Kreisel, who had been reading Laurence's short stories before they appeared in volume form, combined a discussion of them with a notice of *This Side Jordan* and concluded: "Ultimately, what is impressive about her writing is her affirmation, without any sentimentality, of the essential dignity of the human personality. In the finest sense of that word, she is a humanist" (112). These views, on the sureness of Laurence's understanding of voice and its rhythms, and on her essential humanism, are repeated in many later assessments of her work.

The Stone Angel, reviewed widely in Britain and the United States as well as in Canada, added a new dimension of Laurence's works to that which her first four books, all on Africa, had accustomed readers. Here was a comparatively new and comparatively young novelist writing powerfully, at a time of strong national feeling, on themes that were essentially Canadian, even if it was hard to describe her as nationalist in the same sense as, say, Hugh MacLennan. It was appropriate in the circumstances that it was at this time that the first lengthy studies of her achievement appeared. These were Barry Callaghan's essay, "The Writings of Margaret Laurence," which appeared in 1965, and S.E. Read's "The Maze of Life: The Work of Margaret Laurence," which came out a year later. Both of them were descriptive accounts of Laurence's work up to and including *The Stone Angel*, and both were appreciative in tone; they informed Canadians that a writer of major importance had appeared among them, and Read talked of "a greatness not yet fully recognized" (44).

These early studies were followed soon by the first book: Clara Thomas's *Margaret Laurence*, a slight work in McClelland and Stewart's "Canadian Writers" series. Thomas followed this with a rather more substantial work, *The Manawaka World of Margaret Laurence*, in 1975. In the same year Joan Hind-Smith devoted the first third of her *Three Voices* to Laurence, and Patricia Morley's *Margaret Laurence* appeared in 1981. All these books suffer either from brevity, or from a tendency to concentrate on the setting of the novels — the Manawaka world — at the expense of a broad critical analysis. A comprehensive study of her writings in depth remains to be written, as does a biography of her very interesting life.

However, the inadequacies of the existing books and booklets have been partially compensated for by two memorable interviews which Donald Cameron and Graeme Gibson conducted with Margaret Laurence, published in *Conversations with Canadian Novelists* and in *Eleven Canadian Novelists* respectively, in 1973. An even broader view is given in two collections of writing about Margaret Laurence and her work; these are W.H. New's *Margaret Laurence: The Writer and Her Critics* (1977) and my own *A Place to Stand On: Essays by and about Margaret Laurence* (1983). "Margaret Laurence: An Annotated Bibliography" by Susan Warwick appeared in 1979. An interesting development, particularly in view of the relative neglect of her work in Quebec, has been the attention recently paid by French critics to Laurence, which resulted in a whole issue of the journal *Études Canadiennes* being devoted to her work in 1981.

Though no book until the present volume has been devoted to *The Stone Angel* alone, it has been the subject of a number of essays, which increase in complexity from the first brief and somewhat superficial reviews by writers like Robertson Davies and Honor Tracy in 1964. Among the most interesting and the most fruitful

24

suggestions about important elements in Laurence's work and about her affinities with other writers have been made by Sandra Djwa in "False Gods and the True Covenant: Thematic Continuity between Margaret Laurence and Sinclair Ross" (1972); by Clara Thomas in "Pilgrim's Progress: Margaret Laurence and Hagar Shipley" (1981); W.H. New in "Life and Time: Laurence's The Stone Angel" (1972); and "Every Now and Then: Voice and Language in Laurence's *The Stone Angel*" (1983). In addition, there is my own study of archetypal aspects of Laurence's novels, discussed earlier in this chapter, "The Human Elements: Margaret Laurence's Fiction," much of which is devoted to *The Stone Angel*. W.H. New, in his introduction to the New Canadian Library edition of *The Stone Angel* (1968) illuminates the sources and antecedents of the novel, while in his essay on fiction in the *Literary History of Canada*, he places Laurence in the literary context of the Canadian 1960s and 1970s and illuminates the special significance at the time of the first of her Manawaka novels.

Reading of the Text

THE DOUBLE PLOT

The plot of a novel really serves two functions. It is first of all a kind of frame, marking off the shape within which the other elements of fiction, like character and speech and time, develop their patterns. But it really plays a more dynamic role than the frame of a picture. It also operates within the novel as the basic pattern of action, so that it not only establishes the general form of the composition, but — since a novel exists in time in motion whereas a picture exists in time suspended — it also charts the way in which happenings develop out of the interaction of the characters and other factors within the novel. For this reason, while it would be naïve to read a novel merely for the plot or "story" (the record of physical happenings), it would be simplistic to ignore the plot in favour of merely psychological or formal analysis. The novel is not a static form; something always happens within it, and what happens is the plot.

In *The Stone Angel* there are really two interdependent plots. In terms of time present it is the story of an old woman in her nineties whose physical breakdown has made her dependent, and who realizes that her son and daughter-in-law, themselves ageing people, are finding it difficult to look after her at home and are planning to send her to an old-people's institution. Her pride rebels against such an identification with the helpless aged, and one day she escapes from her Vancouver house and her keepers to spend a couple of days in the spartan refuge of an abandoned fish cannery. Inevitably, she is recaptured, alive at least, but somewhat the worse physically for her experience. She is taken, not to the old-people's home, but to a hospital that will be her last home, and where she will have a tenuous experience of fellowship which reveals to her that all her life she has been the victim of her pride. As she says:

26

Pride was my wilderness, and the demon that led me there was fear. I was alone, never anything else, and never free, for I carried my chains within me, and they spread out from me and shackled all I touched. (292)

Shortly afterward she dies, wilfully snatching from the nurse's hands the glass of water "to be had for the taking" that is offered her (308).

But within this primary plot in the present, which lasts only a few days, another plot goes on, as Hagar recollects, in a series of flashbacks, almost the whole of her long life. I use the word "almost," since there is one crucial period of two years that, in contrast to the other vividly remembered periods, goes virtually undescribed. This is the two years when old Jason Currie, Hagar's father, realizing that his two sons are not worth sending to university, decides to spend his money instead on sending Hagar off to what she describes as "the training ring, the young ladies' academy in Toronto"(42). Those years go undescribed in the novel. All we are told is:

When I returned after two years, I knew embroidery, and French, and menu-planning for a five-course meal, and poetry, and how to take a firm hand with servants, and the most becoming way of dressing my hair. Hardly the ideal accomplishments for the kind of life I'd ultimately find myself leading, but I had no notion of that then. (42–43)

What is omitted from a plot is sometimes even more significant than what is put in, and we are left wondering why, while the companions of Hagar's school days in Manawaka play their early roles in the novel (and often, as the years go by, put in an appearance as ageing men and women), there is no mention at all of either Hagar's fellow students, or the teachers who were Hagar's companions during those two years of absence in Toronto. Was the experience so traumatic that it begged to be forgotten? If so, why does Hagar see herself going home as "Pharaoh's daughter returning reluctantly to his roof . . ." (43)?

Certainly, if the two years themselves go untold, their effect is evident throughout the novel. In her long inner monologue Hagar expresses herself in a way quite different from her Manawaka contemporaries and quite unlike Marvin, her son, and his wife Doris, the people to whom in old age her circle has slowly narrowed down. She thinks in an eloquent, vigorous prose, full of vivid imagery, and her mind holds the fragments of what she must have been taught in the "young ladies' academy" like gems from a lost heritage. From the first page one knows that an educated, if no longer disciplined mind is at work in Hagar's gross and worn-out body, for it is no ordinary Manawaka girl who can say of the stone angel which her father erected on her mother's grave:

> I think now she must have been carved in that distant sun by stone masons who were the cynical descendants of Bernini, gouging out her like by the score, gauging with admirable accuracy the needs of fledgling pharaohs in an uncouth land. (3)

An acquired knowledge wedded to a native sense of style must be regarded as the origin of such phrases appearing in the first person narrative, and they are characteristic of Hagar's prose throughout.

Out of those two lost years emerges much that influenced Hagar's inner speech and her ways of thinking. One may speculate also how far her education nurtured in her the strain of Currie pride that makes her defy her strict and stiff-necked father; how far it bred the strain of errant romanticism that leads her to marry the shiftless farmer Bram Shipley; and how far it provoked the restless desire to reshape and refine others that bedevils her marriage, mars her relationship with her sons, and leaves her virtually friendless in the end.

So the plot of *The Stone Angel*, like those of many other works of fiction, keeps something hidden and therefore open to conjecture. In this way it draws readers into the heart of the novel by alerting them to the possibility that Hagar may be telling the truth as she sees it, but it is not necessarily the whole truth. We have to recognize that memories, like opinions, can be biased. All of us, when we think back over our pasts, arrange the untidy chaos that is real life into patterns which may not necessarily be pleasant, but which are certainly more comprehensible than if we tried to remember everything as it actually happened. That is why autobiography is really another kind of fiction.

And that is why, in reading *The Stone Angel*, we have to pay such close attention to the people whom Hagar encounters, even the minor characters who might appear for only a single sentence. It is by observing their reactions, the way they behave to her, the way they speak to her, that we are able to see her as others see her. In this way also we can correct in our minds her self-image that her pride demands, and that makes her so demanding of others. In this way a dimly outlined third plot can be followed in *The Stone Angel*. We read into the behaviour of a bus driver, his mixture of patience and embarrassment, how this ancient adventuring woman must seem to him as she sets off on her attempted escape. And in Marvin's pained laconisms and Doris's whines and covert gestures, we recognize how selfish Hagar's pretensions seem to them, and we see what a burden her pride, even her survival, imposes on others. And we feel for them, as Laurence clearly means us to do. She is "a holy terror" (304), as Marvin remarks, in Hagar's hearing, to one of the nurses in the hospital.

But he says it, as Hagar recognizes, "with such anger and such tenderness" (305), and his confusion anticipates the reader's own ambivalence toward Hagar. For Laurence also means us to feel with Hagar, to catch what is admirable as well as what is pathetic and absurd in her rebellion against age and death. "I feel ambiguous towards her," Laurence said, "because I resent her authoritarian outlook, and yet I love her, too, for her battling" ("Ten Years' Sentences" 15). If she had not wished to arouse this sympathy in us she would hardly have used, as the epigraph to her novel, the lines that Dylan Thomas wrote to his dying father:

> Do not go gentle into that good night.
> Rage, rage against the dying of the light.

We have reached the point where plot merges into character, and I shall be discussing in greater detail later on how Laurence conceived and developed character. But here it is important to note that in all her novels character is really antecedent to plot. The image of the character first emerges in her mind, and action appropriate to the character then determines the plot. Indeed, in "Ten Years' Sentences" she tells us how "the character of Hagar" was present in her mind, and how, once she had "summoned up enough nerve to begin," the novel "wrote itself more easily than anything I have ever done" (13). One assumes from this that the presence of the character and her strength provided the impetus out of which the action developed.

But there are other statements by Laurence which suggest that the development of the plot, and of the themes that go with it, may not have been quite so simple an equation of character and action as the above remarks suggest. Talking to the French critic Michel Fabre, Laurence explained the genesis of *The Stone Angel* in this way:

> For many years I had written not about Canada but Africa where I had been living. And then in some way I had come back to my roots, spiritually, I mean. Even though this return took place at about the same time I returned from Africa, actual geography was less important than this spiritual return out of which, in part, *The Stone Angel* grew. I had started writing on Africa and then I returned to Vancouver and I knew I could not go on writing about Africa. I did not want to. I felt that what I had to do from then on was to write about my own people and culture and geography. Somehow, I did not make a conscious decision, but I felt I would have to start with my grandparents' generation, and Hagar historically belongs to that generation. We generally mostly grew up in a fairly stable, settled community; people knew their grandparents, parents, their own generation, and their children's. Our knowledge is usually limited to four generations. So I thought this was the kind of ancestors I had to begin with, not earlier in history. What was funny with that book is that while I was writing it quite a number of idiomatic expressions came to mind, the way my grandfather would speak, and I didn't even know I had remembered those things. They came out of the filing-cabinet of the mind; this is one thing I felt quite strongly in my case, that I had to go back and write about my own people and country. (203)

Apart from the interesting hints about the way writers approach their subjects, these remarks suggest that it was not entirely a matter of the character of Hagar presenting itself, and the rest of the novel forming about her, as Laurence elsewhere suggests. There seems also to have been a strong urge to recreate the society of her childhood, with its strong generational ties and conflicts; in one sense the plot of *The Stone Angel* can be regarded as a prairie family history. But it is exceptional history, full of negation, of disintegration. For Jason Currie's sons die young and childless and his daughter makes the wrong marriage and is disowned, so that Jason dies in proud and bitter isolation. As for Hagar's personal family, her marriage with

Bram breaks down when she can endure his feckless and vulgar ways no longer and departs, to find her final home in Vancouver. Her beloved son John dies, and it is the son she disregards, Marvin, who becomes the faithful supporter of her old age.

The pattern of flight from Manawaka marks all the novels which begin in that little town, and *A Bird in the House* as well. All their heroines depart to seek themselves in the broader world, and so departure and willing exile are elements that help to shape the action and determine the themes of all these books. But Hagar's exiles are the greatest and most complicated; they include not only those two repressed years at the school in Toronto and the lingering existence in Vancouver that extends from middle age to extreme old age, but also her life with Bram on the farm; for not only by location but also by lifestyle she is self-excluded from the Manawaka of her youth.

All this fits her name, for the Hagar of biblical legend was the handmaiden of Sarah, who bore Abraham his first child, Ishmael, and who was expelled into the desert through Sarah's jealousy. She became an outcast, as her namesake in *The Stone Angel* is cast out by her own pride. And this choice of the name Hagar, whose associations make it an unusual one for a Christian family to give its daughter, provides an interesting link between Margaret Laurence's Canadian novels and her African experiences. It suggests that the break between Africa and Canada in her fiction was not as complete as Laurence herself seems later to have supposed. There is always an underlying continuity in the works of writers if we are willing to take the trouble to seek it out, and there are in fact several features that link *The Stone Angel*, in terms of action and otherwise, to Laurence's preoccupations and experiences while in Africa.

Laurence tells us that when she first went to Africa she read the earlier books of the Bible, notably Genesis, with more attention than ever before, and when she found herself among the desert wanderers of Somaliland it was impossible for her not to relate them to the wandering Israelites and even more to the outcast Hagar and her son Ishmael from whom the Moslems of the desert claimed descent (*The Prophet's* 9). There is a poignant scene in *The Prophet's Camel Bell* that seems to recreate in modern terms the whole legend of the biblical Hagar. It occurs at a time of drought, when Margaret and Jack Laurence are driving through the desert from one of his engineering expeditions:

31

Driving along the Awareh-Hargeise road, we saw two burden camels laden with the crescent-shaped hut-frames and the bundled mats. They were halted by the roadside, and as we drew near, we saw one of the beasts slide to its knees, sunken in the apathy of thirst and exhaustion. Beside them, squatting in the sand, was a woman, a young woman, her black headscarf smeared with dust. She must have possessed, once, a tenderly beautiful face. Now her face was drawn and pinched. In her hands she held an empty tin cup. She did not move at all, or ask for water. Despair keeps its own silence. Her brown robe swayed in the wind. She carried a baby slung across one hip. The child's face was quiet, too, its head lolling in the heavy heat of the sun. We had a little water left in our spare tank, and so we stopped. She did not say a word, but she did something then which I have never been able to forget.

She held the cup for the child to drink first.

She was careful not to spill a drop. Afterwards, she brushed a hand lightly across the child's mouth, then licked her palm so that no moisture would be wasted . . . .

As we drove away, we saw her rise slowly and call the burden camels. The beasts struggled up and began to follow her. (65)

Here was a Hagar in real life, and Laurence remembered her, just as her namesake in the novel must have remembered the biblical Hagar when she thought of herself as a dweller in wildernesses — "Pride was my wilderness" (*The Stone Angel* 292). Even the cup of water returns in the novel, offered to Hagar in her last moment, as it was offered to the woman in the Somali desert in her time of need.

There are other important biblical echoes in *The Stone Angel* which I shall discuss later on; for the moment I am concerned with the disguised ways in which Laurence's African experiences centre the plots of her Canadian novels. Perhaps the most important instance, apart from the recollection of the modern Hagar in the desert, is the stone angel that gives the novel its title.

The stone angel is most important in the novel for its symbolic role. A symbol, according to the *Oxford English Dictionary*, is "a material object representing or taken to represent something immaterial or abstract," and the symbolist writers who appeared in France during the late nineteenth century sought to use objects in their writing to *suggest* ideas and emotions rather than *stating* them directly. Like many modern writers, Margaret Laurence was influenced by symbolism, but used its methods only partially, so that few objects or images in her novels are wholly symbolic; usually they play a part in furthering the action of the novel even when they have a broader function in suggesting leading ideas or evoking certain emotions.

The stone angel is one object which has this double role. It symbolizes Jason Currie's pride when he sets it up, nominally as a monument to his dead wife, but really to "proclaim his dynasty, as he fancied, for ever and a day" (3) — the dynasty that in a bitterly ironic twist of fate expires with him. But it also symbolizes Hagar's blind refusal to recognize her own nature and the consequences of her pride: "She was doubly blind, not only stone but unendowed with even a pretence of sight. Whoever carved her had left the eyeballs blank" (3). And, finally, it symbolizes the way in which — as she realizes while growing older — Hagar shares the obstinate, arrogant disposition of Jason Currie, and even his attitudes to life. Pride is the besetting sin of both of them, which makes them often strangely unfeeling; the idea of those unmoving eyes recurs when Hagar's son John is killed driving a truck over a railway bridge on a dare, and Hagar says: "The night my son died I was transformed to stone and never wept at all" (243).

But the stone angel does not stand always in symbolic isolation from the lives of the characters of the novel it begins and names. At least once it plays an important passive role in the development of the plot. Hagar goes back to the farm outside Manawaka where Bram is slowly dying, and being helped on his way by their son John, who is dosing him with home-brew. One day she insists on going to the cemetery to see if her father's plot has been properly cared for. She finds that the angel has been pushed over, and has fallen on its face. She insists that it be raised, and John grudgingly does this, but when he gets the statue upright Hagar sees to her further horror that its mouth has been smeared with lipstick, which she rubs away in a frenzy lest her old schoolfriends who tend their family graves nearby should see it.

"Who could have done it?" I said. "Who'd do such a wanton thing?"

"How could I know?" John said again. "Some drunk, I guess."

He never said another word about it, although he knew quite well I didn't believe him. (180)

And so another gap that has to be filled with conjecture is opened in the plot of the novel, as the reader weighs John's evasiveness against Hagar's suspicions. But the incident is crucial, because it reveals how much more importance Hagar attributes, despite her defiance of her father Jason, to her family traditions, and it leads up to the point when Bram dies and she insists on putting his name on the Currie tombstone. John now shows his complete detachment from all she stands for: "They're only different sides of the same coin, anyway, he and the Curries. They might as well be together there" (184). Only a little earlier he has shown his indifference to the Currie tradition by trading a family plaid pin for a knife with one of the Tonnerre boys, who belong to a Métis clan that Hagar despises.

These incidents are the beginning of the series of disputes between possessive Hagar and restless John that contribute indirectly to his death. And so the stone angel is not only a symbol, but, like the Commendatore's statue in *Don Giovanni*, plays its malign part in the action of the novel.

Margaret Laurence disclaimed identification of the stone angel with any monument in the cemetery in her home town of Neepawa, though local inhabitants had done their best to name an original. In fact she was right, for the angel was a memory from her first voyage to Africa, when she sailed via Genoa and visited "the Staglieno cemetery, where marble angels loomed like spirits of vengeance among the green-black cypress trees and where the poor rented graves for seven years . . ." (6). The stone angels of Genoa impressed her so much that she not only recorded them in *The Prophet's Camel Bell*, but also brought them into her volume of African stories, *The Tomorrow-Tamer*, where the hairdresser Mr. Archipelago, in "The Perfume Sea," tells one of his customers:

The only place I ever liked in all Genoa was the Staglieno cemetery, up on the hills. I used to go there and sit beside the tombs of the rich, a small fat boy with the white marble angels — so compassionate they looked, and so costly — I believed

34

then that each was the likeness of a lady buried beneath. Then I would look over the fields of rented graves nearby. (25–26)

Likewise, as a child, Hagar found the cemetery at Manawaka, with its single marble angel, a refuge from the less desirable environs of her town.

I used to walk there often when I was a girl. There could not have been many places to walk primly in those days, on paths, where white kid boots and dangling skirts would not be torn by thistles or put in unseemly disarray. (4–5)

And so, just as *The Stone Angel* looked forward to the Manawaka novels, and in some ways set a pattern for them, it also looked back to Margaret Laurence's African experiences and bore their traces.

CHARACTER AND REALISM

Know then thyself, presume not God to scan;
The proper study of mankind is man.

Alexander Pope's couplet might not be acceptable, at least as he wrote it, in our gender-conscious age, but it can be acceptably paraphrased to define the aims of the realistic novel, whose proper subject is humanity: the inner life and outer relations of human beings. One can extend the relevance of Pope's epigram by observing that the acquisition of self-awareness ("Know then thyself") is often the destination of a realistic novel, especially if the novel is written in the first person, and purports to project the inner life of its protagonist-narrator.

In this sense, *The Stone Angel* represents a decisive turning back on Margaret Laurence's part to the best traditions of the realistic novel. In this book she not only distances herself from the didactic concerns of the leading Canadian novelists who had preceded her: the moralistic structures of Morley Callaghan's parable-novels and the nationalistic lessons overtly projected in Hugh MacLennan's long political essays in fiction. She also proceeds beyond her own early fiction, and especially *This Side Jordan,* where the lives of the characters exemplify the difficulties of adjusting to the death of colonialism: the problems of whites resignedly or angrily accepting the end of imperialism and of blacks coping with the challenge of freedom and responsibility.

There are no such didactic goals in *The Stone Angel.* It returns to the terrain of classic realist fiction, whose true aims are the examination of mind and the observation of manners. More specifically, an imaginative record is created of the mental lives of individual men and women, and the way their thoughts and emotions affect their relationships with each other and bring about consequences that are tragic, comic, or ironic, according to the nature of the characters the novelist creates. Thus, while in a novel like Hugh MacLennan's *Barometer Rising* (1941) we follow the development of a theme, the rise of Canadian national consciousness, and the human relationships are subordinate to that theme, in a novel like *The Stone Angel* it is the self-revelation of a person, a character, that dominates our attention.

In this section I propose to discuss three points of view on character in Laurence's novels and especially in *The Stone Angel:* character seen by Laurence as author, character revealed through a reading of the novel itself, and character as perceived by some of the critics who have written on Laurence's work. But I would like to begin with some general observations on the way character can be approached — observations which I think will help to reveal the complexity and sophistication of Laurence's practice.

The conscious development of character in literature goes back at least to the fourth century B.C., when Theophrastus, a pupil of the great philosopher Aristotle, wrote a book called *Characters,* very popular in the ancient world, which consisted of some thirty sketches of types of people who in their behaviour revealed characteristic traits. Shortly afterwards, one of the pupils of Theophrastus, a young man named Menander, took to writing comedies for the Athenian theatre, and used the method of characterization invented by his master to create characters for the stage. Menander's characters tended to be types — the wronged young woman, the tyrannical father, the goldenhearted whore — that were repeated often in the hundred plays he wrote, but they were much more human in the sense of resembling ordinary Athenian citizens than the legendary heroes and heroines in the grand tragedies of Aeschylus and Sophocles and Euripides. In the plays of Menander realistic characterization began, and later dramatists and the novelists who followed them never quite abandoned character-as-type.

Margaret Laurence has certainly created characters who are types as well as individuals. Stacey MacAindra in *The Fire-Dwellers* is, on one level, the type of the frustrated Canadian housewife in whom many women readers see themselves mirrored, and her sister Rachel Cameron is the type of the timid spinster. This aspect is quite apart from the strongly individual sides of their personalities. Readers similarly identified Hagar Shipley as the type of the arrogant old women fighting against age and death. As Laurence herself said, with an expression of surprise that strikes one as a little disingenuous:

> I wrote about Hagar as one individual old woman, who certainly came out of my own background. But I was astonished when a number of other Canadians wrote to me or said to me that this was their grandmother. And I didn't know that it was going to turn out to be everybody's grandmother. (Kroetsch 48)

Closely related to the Theophrastian character-as-type was the concept of the character as humour, very fashionable in Elizabethan drama and most brilliantly exemplified in the plays of Ben Jonson. As I have already explained, the humours were really a method of classifying human temperaments in relation to the ancient concept of the four elements. The heroines of Laurence's four major novels can each be seen as an example of one of the classic humours — Stacey: sanguine, Rachel: phlegmatic, Morag: melancholic, and Hagar, with her recurrent angers at people and at fate, as the victim of her own choleric nature.

Another concept of character that has had considerable attention from critics is the idea of the character as persona. The word persona, of course, originally meant a mask. Some of this sense of concealment has continued into the later usage, which suggests that a character in a novel is a guide for him- or herself that the writer develops from some aspect of his or her own personality. This undoubtedly happens with writers who are not particularly inventive and are also self-obsessed; Malcolm Lowry's major characters, for example, are obviously projections of various aspects of his own complex nature. But Laurence has declared emphatically that, so far as she is concerned, "[T]he character is not a mask, but an individual, separate from the writer" ("Time" 156). And, though the character of the writer Morag Gunn in *The Diviners* does seem to share aspects of a personality as well as a profession with her creator, one can accept the disclaimer so far as the earlier novels are concerned. Hagar Shipley in *The Stone Angel* is in no sense a projection of the Laurence who wrote *The Stone Angel*, though something of the way the novelist imagined growing old may have entered into her empathetic view of Hagar's predicament.

Yet there is another sense in which the mask does play its part in the characterization of the Manawaka novels: each of them is at one level concerned with the problem of appearances, and we are very clearly shown the guises through which the bewildered real selves of Laurence's characters look out on the world. In every case there is a concealed self, sustained by a flow of memory and inner monologue. But there is also a mask that is always worn when a character moves in the world, which is seen as a place where beings masked by prejudice and fear confront each other and occasionally drop their guises and come together in freedom and love. Hagar Shipley is constantly engaged in this play of appearances and masks herself not only from the people she knows but also from herself, so that some of the most important turning points in the novel come when she is forced into self-recognition.

One such incident occurs after she has been vegetating on the farm and, without realizing it, has been sinking to Bram Shipley's level of squalid living. One day she goes into Manawaka with the eggs she sells on the side to make a little pocket money. She calls at a house where the daughter shouts: "Mother, the egg woman's here!" and her old and once despised schoolmate Lottie Simmons comes to the door. Something in Lottie's look penetrates her defence of indifference, and she hurries off immediately to the town's rest room:

I had never been inside it, not fancying public conveniences. But I told John to let me off there that night. One room it was, with brown wainscoting and half a dozen straight chairs, and the two toilet cubicles beyond. No one was there. I made sure of that before I entered. I went in and found what I needed, a mirror. I stood for a long time, looking, wondering how a person could change so much and never see it. So gradually it happens.

I was wearing, I saw, a man's black overcoat that Marvin had left. It was too big for John and impossibly small for Bram. It still had a lot of wear left in it, so I'd taken it. The coat bunched and pulled up in front, for I'd put weight on my hips, and my stomach had never gone flat again after John was born. Twined around my neck was a knitted scarf, hairy and navy blue, that Bram's daughter Gladys had given me one Christmas. On my head a brown tam was pulled down to keep my ears warm. My hair was grey and straight. I always cut it myself. The face — a brown and leathery face that wasn't mine. Only the eyes were mine, staring as though to pierce the lying glass and get beneath to some truer image, infinitely distant. (133)

What the mirror tells Hagar leads to action, to a major shift in her life, for she decides to put an end to her servitude to Bram and his decrepit farm, sells her heirlooms to Lottie Simmons so that she can buy herself some good clothes, and goes to Vancouver. There she becomes housekeeper to the old merchant Mr. Oatley, and they live for the time being a perfect masked existence: "Mr. Oatley never questioned me, nor I him, and we lived there amicably, keeping a suitable distance from one another" (158). But Hagar, looking back, realizes that despite such intervals of successfully guarded existence, she is not impervious to the shocks of life. She says: "It was a becalmed life we led there, a period of waiting and of marking time. But the events we waited for, unknowingly, turned out to be quite other than what I imagined they might be" (160). These events, which rudely strip the mask away, are Bram's final sickness, which takes Hagar back to Manawaka; his death; and, not very long afterwards, the death of her son John. This last isolates Hagar in a sorrow she cannot express, and so leaves her to the life of pride and antagonism with which she lives into her angry old age.

All these aspects of character — as type, as humour, and as mask — thus find their places in Margaret Laurence's characterization of Hagar. But she insists that Hagar is something more than the sum of such traditional elements, and what she presents, based on her own experience as a novelist, is a vision of the virtually organic development of a character who, as she says, is "not a mask, but an individual, separate from the writer" ("Time" 186). The relationship between writer and character as she presents it has strongly Jungian undertones, for she talks of the emergence of a character in the writer's mind almost as if it were the visitation of an archetype emerging from the unconscious: "I did not consciously choose any particular time in history, or any particular characters. The reverse seemed to be true. The character of Hagar in *The Stone Angel* seemed almost to choose me" ("A Place" 16).

In her essay "Time and the Narrative Voice," Laurence has some especially pertinent things to say about the relationship between her kind of writer and the characters she creates. She takes off from her denial that the character is a mask of the writer by making the significant admission that:

> At the same time, the character is one of the writer's voices and selves, and fiction writers tend to have a mental trunkful of these — in writers, this quality is known as richness of imagination; in certain inmates of mental hospitals it has other names, the only significant difference being that writers are creating their private worlds with the ultimate hope of throwing open the doors to other humans. This means of fiction, oriented almost totally towards an individual character, is obviously not the only way, but it appears to be the only way I can write. ("Time" 156)

And a little later on she reinforces these remarks with a passage which clearly shows her sense of characters as entities that have taken on autonomous existences; they are out there and clamouring to enter. The writer can *know* them as persons separate from herself; know them:

> so well that one can take on their past, their thoughts, their responses, can in effect for a while *become* them. It has sometimes occurred to me that I must be a kind of Method writer, in the same way that some actors become the characters they play for the moments when they are portraying these characters. I didn't plan it this way, and possibly it sounds like gibberish, but this is how it appears to take place. ("Time" 156)

What Laurence is saying here is actually borne out by the experience of many writers. There is a touch of the schizoid in the mind of any writer — whether of fiction or drama — who deals with the creation of characters that seem to the readers to be convincing human beings. That, of course, was what Gustave Flaubert meant when he made his celebrated remark, itself an implicit manifesto of fictional realism: "Madame Bovary, c'est moi." Even biographers can have — and the best of them do have — the sense while they are writing that they become in a way the people they have chosen as their subjects. I can vouch for this from experience. When I was writing a life of the French anarchist Pierre-Joseph Proudhon, I felt such a close identity with him that I not only found myself thinking like Proudhon but I also detected my body mimicking his physical states; before the book was finished I was suffering badly from the asthma of which he died, though I have never been asthmatic before or since. On another occasion, when I wrote my biography of the great Métis leader Gabriel Dumont (whom Laurence admired), I was astonished by the ease with which I entered into the feelings and motives of a man whose background and life had been utterly different from my own. In that instance the degree of imaginative insight I acquired allowed me to present Dumont in a way that made him so similar to a character in a novel that the novelist Matt Cohen complimented me on the *fictional* feeling of my biography.

I make this personal diversion merely to confirm from my own experience the degree to which writers become possessed by their characters, and often seem to be writing according to the dictates of these beings who live only in their minds, so that, as Laurence said:

Characters take off and appear to be acting quite under their own motivations, which in fact they are. That is what I think of as a kind of direct connection with the characters. You don't have any control really over what happens to them. (Kroetsch 50–51)

Here we are dealing with the mysteries of creation, and it is time we got back to *The Stone Angel* and to character as it emerges there. Here the key phrase from the previous passages by Margaret Laurence is that in which she tells us that "[T]his means of fiction, always oriented towards an individual character" is the only way in which she can write ("Time" 156). And, indeed, one of the most striking features of the Manawaka novels (and also of the linked stories in *A Bird in the House*), is that they centre on the inner life of a single main character and her progress toward some kind of self-knowledge and hence toward some kind of reconciliation with life, no matter how late and equivocal, as is the case with Hagar Shipley.

All of the Manawaka novels follow this pattern of concentrating on an individual character, always a woman. This is in contrast to the pattern of Laurence's African novel, *This Side Jordan*, in which we are equally concerned with the problematic lives of a number of characters, who assume more or less equal importance, and whose interaction thus creates a dramatic dialogue. By abandoning this multivocal pattern and concentrating on a single perceiving and experiencing being, the author automatically creates certain limitations which she challenges herself to turn into strengths. To begin with, there is only one point of view to which we have primary access, in the case of *The Stone Angel*, that of Hagar. Because Laurence is not writing a solipsistic stream-of-consciousness novel, but a first-person narrative of encounters in the "real" world, we are not cut off from collective experience. Indeed, Laurence has always stressed the social nature of her perceptions. She once described *The Stone Angel* as "the first book of mine written out of my own culture and people" (Sullivan 62). Manawaka, the community, is a notable creation; it takes on character of its own by osmosis from the characters of its inhabitants and embodies the collective mores against which the characters react. Nevertheless, while the public opinion of Manawaka is undoubtedly a presence in all of Laurence's Canadian novels, and its structure of cliques and classes and ethnic groups (the dominant Scots versus the Ukrainians and the Métis) are factors in determining what happens with them, we only become aware of them insofar as they impinge on the lives of the leading characters and are filtered through their awarenesses.

In the same way, the Manawaka novels are filled with characters of varying importance in relation to the heroines, who are usually presented in such a way that they are highly individual and often memorable. Indeed, there are some, such as Christy in *The Diviners*, who are so filled with Dickensian vitality that they threaten temporarily to divert our attention from the central character. Yet we are always aware of them only because of their relationship to that central character. We are never allowed to look directly into the minds of Jason Currie or Bram Shipley in *The Stone Angel*; we see them only through Hagar's eyes, hear them through her ears, and know what she chooses to let us know about them. Since Hagar has a flair for eloquent description (presumably acquired during those two lost years in Toronto), we are often given a fairly vivid description of their appearance and their eccentricities, and we even gain some idea of their special ways of speaking. Hagar is not allowed to turn them into mere puppets in her memory or her imagination. Yet always she shows them as her foils, the *others* by whom, in her great egotism, she defines herself, and she never has an unreservedly good word to say about any of them. They are, irrevocably, minor figures in Hagar's vision of her life. Consequently, while the book has its tragic aspects — for Hagar's flaws of character have undoubtedly helped to give her life its unhappy direction — there is no real drama since there is no real dialogue. The characters never truly converse; they exchange statements that are embedded in the great sprawling continuum of Hagar's memory, and their encounters are stylized in recollection like the encounters of romances. Everything we know about them is secondary, filtered through the principal character's thoughts.

And so, as in all first-person novels, we come to the question of how far we can trust this narrator who is telling us about her own life. This is a subject that critics relish. In the case of one famous Canadian prairie novel, Sinclair Ross's *As for Me and My House*, the narrator is an aggrieved wife who always speaks with the voice of saddened reason. The earliest readers of the book tended to take her narrative at face value, since she seemed such an understanding, reasonable and forgiving woman. But later critics have argued that in Mrs. Bentley's sweet reasonableness a great hypocrisy is concealed, and that we must regard her account as self-serving, however she may have concealed her bias. Since Ross has never pronounced on this difficult issue, the controversy goes on.

This controversy does not arise in the case of Hagar Shipley. Her prejudices and her resentments stand out for all to see, and we are on guard all the time for the bias that sooner or later emerges in all her statements. Her fear and suspicion of the world colour her relationships with everyone. For example, she describes a situation early in the book but late in her life, where she is sitting at tea with her son Marvin and his wife Doris.

"Care for a little more lemon slice, Mother?"
Why is he so attentive? I watch their faces. Does a questioning look pass between them or do I only fancy it is so?
"No, thank you, Marvin." Aloof. Alert. Not to be taken in. (34)

43

As things turn out, Hagar has reason to be alert, since Marvin and Doris are thinking about putting her in a home. But the suspicion that divides her from other people is obviously not new. Yet here the reader faces another problem. The story of Hagar's past, as it appears in the alternating chapters, is vividly presented. We see everything with a preternatural clarity, whether it is the scenes of Hagar's girlhood or the lush and intricate flora and fauna of the forest around the fish cannery where she goes on her last escapade. But we all know that very old people remember the distant past with great vividness, and this is clearly what Hagar is doing, for her memories effectively end when John is killed, somewhere in the depression years, a quarter of a century before the present of the novel.

But are the memories of old people — or any memories, however vivid — the real past? The French novelist Marcel Proust argued that the imagination plays an active part in remembering, and that our recollections are in fact a selection and rearrangement of incidents and impressions from the past. Thus, in all works of fiction that are based on remembering the past, we must regard memory itself as the first creator of fiction, even before the novelist gets to work. After all, the important fact about Hagar (as Laurence has repeated again and again), is that she is an old woman of ninety. It is an old woman's voice we hear, preserving the way of speech of her youth (and of Laurence's grandparents' days), but remembering as old people do and perhaps even taking the process a stage further by mentally editing the memories as they occur to her. It is, I suggest, a novel about Hagar and her old woman's memories rather than a novel about Hagar and her past.

But, whatever that past may really have been, it has made her into what she is, the woman whose voice is brilliantly introduced in the first pages of the novel, describing the stone angel, referring somewhat contemptuously to the inhabitants of the cemetery where it stands, and evoking the undisciplined assault of nature on this haven of respectful memory:

> But sometimes through the hot rush of disrespectful wind that
> shook the scrub oak and the coarse couchgrass encroaching
> upon the dutifully cared-for habitations of the dead, the scent of
> the cowslips would rise momentarily. They were tough-rooted,
> these wild and gaudy flowers, and although they were held back

at the cemetery's edge, torn out by loving relatives determined to keep the plots clear and clearly civilized, for a second or two a person walking there could catch the faint, musky, dust-tinged smell of things that grew untended and had grown always, before the portly peonies and the angels with rigid wings, when the prairie bluffs were walked through only by Cree with enigmatic faces and greasy hair. (5)

Enigmatic faces and greasy hair! Here she expresses the part-admiration for the lingering myth of the noble savage, and part-contempt for real Indians, which in the rest of the novel Hagar extends to the Métis. The tone is already set throughout the passage for the ambivalence of Hagar's memories, the alternation that runs through her life between rebellion and conformity, both of which are emanations of her pride. Her pride, in its turn, has a paradoxical quality, for, as Clara Thomas has said: "Hagar Shipley is sustained by her pride and she is made monstrous by her pride." She is "humiliated hourly and daily" by the vulnerability her age has imposed on her. But, Thomas continues:

in the unbending pride of her spirit there is also enormous strength: she journeys through memory to one last, brief and desperate bid for escape from the chains of age and illness. She comes to her final hospital bed, but she also comes to her moment of truth and liberation, the recognition of the force that warped her own life and her love for others. ("Pilgrim's Progress" 160–61)

That force is pride.

Yet, as W.H. New has remarked, the novel ends with a deliberate uncertainty that has perhaps nothing to do with Hagar as a character, if we conceive character in the sense of earthly being, of a mind within a palpable today. New says:

And Hagar herself, at the end of the book, is also as defiant as ever. She has discovered who she is, discovers that she is alone; there is no greater tragedy for her, and yet no greater satisfaction. Her final words, "And then —," uttered in the novel at the time of her death, are part of a chronology and therefore part of time. But by leaving the sentence unfinished, Mrs. Laurence closes the book in ambivalence; it is possible that time stops, but possible also that it goes on, and is merely measured in a different way. (Introduction, *The Stone Angel* x)

For we have to remember that, although Hagar may have abandoned the religion of her childhood, Laurence remained a believing Christian to the end of her life, even if her ethics may have been stronger than her theology. She leaves no doubt that Hagar's pride is the spiritual pride that was regarded as one of the seven deadly sins by the medieval theologians. In the unorthodox way that things always happen to her, Hagar goes through her last rite for the living when Mr. Troy, the minister, sings "All people that on earth do dwell," and her act of contrition is her realization that she has not recognized the need for joy. At that moment her mind is enlightened and her heart opened. We are not told, but perhaps we can surmise that her snatching of the cup of water in her last moment is a symbol of her release from the agony of memory into the great peace beyond life.

AN ARCHITECTURE OF TIME

Since novels, unlike short stories, are concerned with time as continuity rather than time as the halted moment, the temporal nature of a work has become increasingly important to authors during recent years. They have been encouraged in this preoccupation by the speculation on the nature of time that has figured so greatly in nineteenth- and twentieth-century philosophical writings, and by the original speculation on the relationship between time and space that emerged as Albert Einstein developed his theory of relativity. In fact, time, as a fourth dimension, offered a new space for fiction to explore.

Early fictional narrative had been essentially sequential, events following each other as they do in our daily physical lives. The first novels, those of Defoe, for instance, were concealed biographies, in which men and women were born, lived, and died, according to biological rhythms of growth and decay. But as fiction writers became increasingly concerned with the inner lives of their characters, and were encouraged in this by advances in psychology, they were forced to recognize that the time of the mind is not necessarily the same as the time of the body. We are aware of the body's time ticking away in heartbeats like a clock, and the events we physically experience take their place within that sphere of bodily time. But in our minds we are outside that process much of the time; we are remembering the past, we are fantasizing about the future; if we are mystically inclined we may have the sense of slipping out of time entirely. Even if we are not, there are still our dreams in which we live in a world where ordinary concepts of time and space have lost relevance, where the dead can live and the past can merge into a future that will perhaps never come into being in the physical world, the world of clocks. Which time is true time? The question is still unanswered.

For generations now, novelists have been trying to deal with this volatility of internal time. One of the great pioneer efforts was Marcel Proust's massive novel sequence, fifteen volumes long, which he called *À la recherche du temps perdu*. The English version is called *Remembrance of Things Past*, a title that misses the true meaning of the original, whose intent can best be expressed by a more literal translation, "In search of lost time"; for it is to studying what happens when the mind seeks out the past through memory that Proust devotes his masterpiece.

Proust's pioneering work caused a revolution in realist fiction. The theoretical aim of realism, as distinct from fantasy literature of various kinds, has been to portray, with the greatest possible honesty, things as they are. One of the early realist novelists, William Godwin, actually used the subtitle "Things as They Are" for his best-known novel, *The Adventures of Caleb Williams*. But realist novelists ran into two difficulties, both of which are reflected in the problems that Margaret Laurence encountered in writing *The Stone Angel* and which readers sometimes experience in coming to terms with the book.

The first is the virtual impossibility of presenting life as it is. Historians, as well as novelists, are faced with the uncomfortable fact that life — individual life and public life — is a chaos of episodes and impressions so intricate that to record it as it is experienced would involve amassing vast chronicles of details, most of which would in the end seem irrelevant. It would seem irrelevant because human beings, even if they are not novelists or artists of any kind, have a natural tendency — which seems built into the structure of the mind — to order the data of experience into patterns which correspond to their personal myths, or their ideas of who they are and what the purpose of their lives should be. Like Hagar Shipley, we all look at life with a bias that is natural to us, and indeed is part of our individuality. What we remember and even perceive is what seems relevant to our view of our lives and our world. This applies alike to our memories, our perceptions of the present, and our ideas about the future, all of which influence the way we look at both past and present.

If you and I, in the years of our lives, find it necessary to select and arrange the data of experience to make sense out of our pasts, it is obvious that writers setting out with two or three hundred pages to create the convincing image of a life, or even art of a life, will be forced to select their happenings and fit them into an appealing pattern. In doing so, they will be satisfying that desire for form which all human beings seem to share.

And the conscious search for and achievement of significant form is, of course, what we mean by art. As Laurence herself remarks of the problems she encountered in writing *The Stone Angel*: "writing, however consciously unordered its method — is never as disorderly as life. Art, in fact, is never life. It is never as paradoxical, chaotic, complex or as alive as life" ("Gadgetry" 83). In other words, the old goal of realism, to portray "things as they are," has always been a mirage. Realism is another literary convention whose particular trick is to give the illusion of authenticity. Like any other kind of writing, it achieves this end and satisfies our desire for meaningful form by the use of artifice. It does not present a literal likeness of life, but creates a kind of model in the imagination that helps us to understand life. And our changed understanding of the complexity of time perception has presented realist novelists with a second crucial problem — the search for a way of presenting a model of the actual experience of time as distinct from the way we see it on the dials of clocks and watches, which has now become one of the goals of literary realism.

In the last section I touched on time in my discussion of the ways in which Laurence's articulation of memory illuminates the character of Hagar Shipley. Now, to the discussion of architecture of *The Stone Angel*, time and memory return, but in a different way. In fact, it is an enhanced view of the importance of these elements which distinguishes Laurence's Canadian fiction from her African fiction. This is a result of a shift in the experiential basis of her novels, for though she has always insisted that she never took a character from life, she has certainly taken the human data on which her novels are based from life, well lived and sensitively perceived.

This Side Jordan not only dealt with the relationships between its characters during a short time of dramatic change; it was also the product of observations which Margaret Laurence had made over a brief period in a place where she had no roots and therefore no sense of personal immersion in the past. For it was a past which belonged to others and not to her; she would always remain, as she often emphasized, a "stranger" in Africa. And so, while she does not entirely ignore the earlier lives of her characters, her point of perception for the third-person narrative is in the present.

Time took on different meaning as soon as Laurence returned home and began to write of her own country and her own region. The ancient Hagar who haunted her imagination connoted, among other things, ancestry, and her novels were written within a time continuum that embraced the whole history of her imaginary community of Manawaka and the four generations of prairie Canadians she had known. The question of how to move within that continuum has tended to dominate the structures of her novels ever since, and it was in her exploration of ways to deal fictionally with time that Margaret Laurence showed an experimental side to her view of the objectives of fiction, which in general had been somewhat conservatively realistic.

Thus in her Manawaka novels, and especially in *The Stone Angel*, time is the most important factor in determining the structure (though the continuum of this novel is genuinely four-dimensional, since space does play its vital role). Manawaka is not a sealed community, and though people born there may feel its isolation and wish to depart, as Laurence herself longed to depart from Neepawa, it is only their own fear of the tempting world outside that holds them there. In the same way Rachel Cameron in *A Jest of God* is held by the self-imposed spell of her timidity until she finally releases herself. So all the heroines eventually depart, and the destination they share, even if some of them go farther, is Vancouver. Here the lush and temperate coast with its cosmopolitan population and its easy lifestyle is the most extreme contrast in Canada to the aridity, the climactic rigours, the closed society, and the social and ethnic prejudices of Manawaka and the prairie communities it represents. Manawaka haunts the memories of these escapees, but they only return at times of crisis and usually when someone in the ancestral sequence has died. And so time watches over their arrivals and departures, and asserts itself over the spatial patterns as the dominant structural element.

The assertion of temporal dominance occurs a number of times in the novel. Hagar, leaving Bram, and at the same time leaving her home town, comments on her departure: "Then we were away from Manawaka. It came as a shock to me, how small the town was, and how short a time it took to leave it, as we measure time" (147). It is through her sense of time that Hagar measures the space of Manawaka. And then, coming to Vancouver, she voices a sentiment, to be repeated in different ways by other Manawaka heroines making their escapes:

> To move to a new place — that's the greatest excitement. For a while you believe you carry nothing with you — all is canceled from before, or cauterized, and you begin again and nothing will go wrong this time. (155)

Not "nothing will go wrong in this place," but "nothing will go wrong this time." For it is time, not place, that manifests itself in change, particularly since the real changes in Laurence's novels come from within, arising from a change of mind or heart rather than a change of place, and time is mind's dimension.

Though its language and its imagery give *The Stone Angel* a sense of verbal richness, or largeness of vision, in terms of action this is a book of narrow compass, the narrative of an old woman's thoughts and memories on the eve of death, with a single Quixotic escapade, the flight to the fish cannery, to break the pattern. Death circumscribes the whole pattern, for the novel begins with memories of a cemetery and ends with Hagar's last expectant thought — "And then — ."

And yet within it are contained, as we have seen, two interlocking plots of considerable power. In one of them, which with some levity one might call "Hagar's Last Stand," a proud and obdurate woman makes her reckoning with decay and death, never submitting, yet in her own proud and grudging way reconciled. And in the other the same old woman traces in her memory the years of the past — but only those that have brought her to this point.

Before examining the structure within which this is achieved, we should consider a caveat which Laurence issues in her essay "Time and the Narrative Voice." Talking about the "treatment of time and the handling of the narrative voice," she remarks that "[i]t is the character who chooses which parts of the personal past, the family past and the ancestral past have to be revealed in order for the present to be realized and the future to happen" (156).

We have already seen Laurence talking about the autonomy of the character; how, once conceived, he or she will go his or her own way, by which she may mean that with her, once it is started, a novel takes on a kind of impetus of its own. She has also said that *The Stone Angel*, once begun, "wrote itself more easily than anything I have ever done." But now she is suggesting something more than this upsurge of inspiration from the unconscious. She is giving the character control of handling time, the most important element in a Laurence novel.

And though we may protest that the character is after all the creation of the author, it does take on, as Laurence suggested, the role of an alternative self to the author, developing, if it is to be credible, in its own special and self-consistent way. And we must further admit that, once the author has conceived of the character and allowed him or her to tell a personal story in the first person, then for the novel itself to be consistent, everything must be presented from that character's special point of view. And that certainly happens in *The Stone Angel*; we hear it all in Hagar's voice, we recognize her voice, and we know that, even in her inner monologue, she is offering only what she chooses to draw from memory.

Nevertheless, however much the tone and the choice of incident in the book may derive from the temperament of the character, it is the writer who decides the broader matters of structure and approach, the architecture of the work. As Laurence says of her own choices regarding *The Stone Angel*:

I decided I would have to write it in the present tense, with flashbacks in the past tense. The method seems a little rigid, but I was dealing with a very rigid character. I did not really like the flashback method much, and God knows it has been over-worked — which is probably why fewer and fewer writers use it now. But I could not discover any alternative which would convey the quality and events of Hagar's long past. In a sense, I think this method works not too badly in *The Stone Angel* simply because Hagar *is* so old, *is* living largely in her past, *does* — like many old people — remember the distant past better than recent events. ("Gadgetry" 83)

The novel consists of alternating passages from a past and a present both of which exist within Hagar's mind; either she is remembering, or she is perceiving the world around her with an old person's suspicious eye which gives her observations their special twist and colour. It opens with Hagar recalling the stone angel in her rich and racy inner prose, the prose of thoughts we are expected to believe are addressed to us. And then, after she has described the cemetery, and we have some handle on her past, she switches to the present. In a paragraph dense with appropriate facts, and vibrant with Hagar's contemptuous attitude and sarcastic voice, she establishes the basic situation of the novel so adroitly and completely that it is worth quoting entirely as an example of how concisely a good novelist can bring the reader into the heart of her material:

Now I am rampant with memory. I don't often indulge in this, or not so very often, anyway. Some people will tell you that the old live in the past — that's nonsense. Each day, so worthless really, has a rarity for me lately. I could put it in a vase and admire it, like the first dandelions, and we would forget their weediness and marvel that they were there at all. But one dissembles, usually, for the sake of such people as Marvin, who is somehow comforted by the picture of old ladies feeding like docile rabbits on the lettuce leaves of other times, other manners. How unfair I am. Well, why not? To carp like this — it's my only enjoyment, that and the cigarettes, a habit I acquired only ten years ago, out of boredom. Marvin thinks it disgraceful of me to smoke at my age, ninety. To him there is something distressing in the sight of Hagar Shipley, who by some mischance happens to be his mother, with a little white burning tube held saucily between arthritic fingers. Now I light one of my cigarettes and stump around my room, remembering furiously, for no reason except that I am caught up in it. I must be careful not to speak aloud, though, for if I do Marvin will look at Doris and Doris will look meaningfully at Marvin, and one of them will say, "Mother's having one of her days." Let them talk. What do I care now what people say? I cared too long. (5–6)

The whole situation of Hagar's present is there, neatly bracketed between an opening reference to memory and a closing reference to the past which alert us to the other dimension of the novel.

From this point until about the last fifth of the book, *The Stone Angel* maintains parallel chronological patterns, the present following sequentially the last days of Hagar's life, and the flashbacks following, also sequentially, the course of her life as it appears in her memories. As we have seen, there is one gap, which Laurence has never explained, in the earlier part of Hagar's life, when Jason Currie sends her off to the young ladies' finishing school in Toronto, and there is a period of perhaps thirty years of Hagar's ageing life that is indicated with the most meagre of memories.

The last significant memory is in fact of the death of Hagar's son John and his lover Arlene, which occurs to her about four-fifths of the way through the novel, during her escapade in the fish cannery. The last chapters of the book are almost wholly concerned with the final days of Hagar's life, and take place mainly in the hospital, where in a number of ways Hagar's pride and isolation are broken down, and she becomes part of a community of sufferers. It is almost as if the years in between have been unlived. John dies in the early 1930s during the depression, and though no sharp dates are given, we can assume that Hagar was then around sixty; thirty years intervene between the end of that past and the present in which Hagar remembers it. But all we are told — and that baldly — is of Hagar's employer, Mr. Oatley, dying and leaving her enough money to buy a house. And then her imagination is struck by the news of the war, when so many Manawaka boys joined up and died at Dieppe. This moves her to think: "He might have been killed or saved. Who's to know? Or do such things depend on what goes on outside?" (244). There is no more, at least in conscious memory; the inner narrative has ended. But a little later, lying in the cannery among the fish boxes, Hagar hallucinates and thinks that Murray F. Lees, the drunken former evangelist who has joined her in her place of escape, is her son

John, and she begs his forgiveness. It is Lees who, recognizing her condition, offers the pardon she has secretly wanted all these long years.

"It's okay," he says. "I knew all the time you never meant it. Everything is all right. You try to sleep. Everything's quite okay." (248)

And so Lees, who in his own strange way was once a man of God, offers her one of her spiritual needs, which is forgiveness, while later on at the hospital, the novel's other man of God, the timid young minister Troy, offers her reconciliation and joy as he sings, in his astonishingly firm and clear voice, "All People that on Earth Do Dwell."

Whether during those long years of growing old, Hagar remembered her past as she does during the brief present of the novel, we are never told. It is possible that Laurence means us to see her memories as a strange efflorescence of her final days, rather like the splendid and desperate flowering that some old trees achieve just before they die. Certainly her main impression of the intervening years seems to be one of dismal and resentful living, at virtual enmity with the world.

I have lived with Marvin and Doris — or they have lived in my house, whichever way one cares to phrase it — for seventeen years. Seventeen — it weighs like centuries. How have I borne it? How have they? (37)

The way Laurence has ordered the lived present and the remembered past in *The Stone Angel* is of course a prime example of the impossibility of literal realism. She herself played the devil's advocate regarding her novel in an interview with Rosemary Sullivan, when she remarked:

my sense of it is that the way people remember is not the way that it happens in *The Stone Angel*, because people's memories don't come along conveniently in a chronological way. But on the other hand, dealing with the life of a very old woman, if I had done it any other way, I felt it would have been tremendously confusing. (76)

54

What she is really telling us is that memory partakes of the chaos of life. We remember sporadically, often in response to chance stimuli — a word spoken or something seen or smelt or tasted — that sets the recollections going in our mind. It is only if we make some kind of deliberate effort, like writing an autobiography, that memories emerge in chronological order in response to a special demand of the mind. The demand Laurence made on the material of memory was a rather similar one, for she wanted the memories to chart a life, and the pattern she gave the novel did precisely that. But her less than complete satisfaction with the result is evident in the fact that in her later novels, though they are all as much concerned with time and memory as *The Stone Angel*, she handles time more experimentally and orders her characters' memories in other ways than the chronologically sequential.

Yet if we are willing to make what Coleridge called "that willing suspension of disbelief for the moment, which constitutes poetic faith," and to see the succession of memories and events through Laurence's and through Hagar's eyes, the pattern may become acceptable. W.H. New has remarked on Hagar's special way of looking at time, a subjective one that really eliminates the distinction between past and present and may be the consequence of her very old age.

> Throughout Hagar's quest to relive the moments that have eluded her and to stave off the moment that awaits her, she thinks of her past life not as *then* but as something interpenetrating *now*: as something ongoing, as a body of moments of transformation. ("Every Now and Then" 190)

But beyond Hagar's outlook, in which our normal conceptions of time are shredding away under the pressure of age, the "willing suspension of disbelief," which is the necessary beginning of any understanding of literature, is facilitated in other ways during our reading of *The Stone Angel*. There are, to begin with, the associative leaps of thought by which the novel moves from present into past and back into present. Sometimes it is possessions which Hagar has accumulated that set her mind moving backward, and often in devious ways, as early in the book, when — after an acrid exchange with Doris — she retreats into her room, to the objects that "support and comfort me."

The gilt-edged mirror over the mantel is from the Currie house. It used to hang in the downstairs hall, where the air was astringent with mothballs hidden under the blue roses of the carpet, and each time I passed it I would glance hastily, not wanting to be seen looking, and wonder why Dan and Matt inherited her daintiness while I was big-boned and husky as an ox. (59)

The mirror sets her thinking vaguely about a dimly seen past, her mother, her brothers. But it is the portrait that plunges her into the real past, fully remembered.

Yet there's the picture of me at twenty. Doris wanted to take it down, but Marvin wouldn't let her — that was a curious thing, now I come to think about it. I was a handsome girl, a handsome girl, no doubt of that. A pity I didn't know it then. Not beautiful, I admit, not that china figurine look some women have, all gold and pink fragility, a wonder their corsets don't snap their sparrow bones. Handsomeness lasts longer, I will say that.

Sometimes these delicate-seeming women can turn out to be quite robust after all, though. (59–60)

And all at once, after a moment of self-flattering contemplation of the artifacts, we are off into the past itself, her brother Matt's wife, and Matt's death, and her unforgiving father of whom all the possessions in some way or another remind her.

Or sometimes it is a mere word floating in her mind. She goes for an x-ray, and is touched by a doctor's gentle remark.

So sudden is his gentleness that it accomplishes the opposite of what he intended and now I'm robbed even of endurance and can only lean here mutely, waiting for whatever they'll perform upon me. (111–12)

It is *waiting* — the word in her mind and then the idea — that sets her off on her next bout of recollection:

I've waited like this, for things to get better or worse, many and many a time. I should be used to it. So many years I waited at the Shipley place — I've almost lost count of them. (112)

And we are back in the bitter, obstinate, often silent conflict between feckless Bram and ridden Hagar fifty years ago.

56

Linked with this there is the other dramatic association, when, having resolved to escape from Marvin and Doris to the fish cannery, and made her elaborate plans, Hagar lapses into a recollection of the time she and John escaped from Bram and the situation on the farm. We realize that the second escape, by starting Hagar's liberation from the pride that imprisons her, will be the successful one (despite its apparent failure in her recapture).

As well as these transitions by association that move us forward through time, there are other connections in *The Stone Angel* by which past loops into the present, and different parts of the past loop into each other. In her interview with Laurence, Rosemary Sullivan remarks:

> I've always felt that your novels work in patterns, not superimposed symbols; characters are often able to liberate themselves from the deadlocks in which they get trapped, by acting out rituals. For instance, in *The Stone Angel*, Hagar cannot release her dying brother from his agony by wearing her mother's shawl, and comforting him, because it would be a lie — at the end of the novel she is allowed to relive this scene symbolically when she finally lies for Marvin.

Laurence replies rather evasively to this question, though she admits to having "quite a strong sense of ritual" (66–67).

But there is no doubt that what Sullivan calls "symbolical repetition" does happen in the novel; the juxtaposition of the two escapes which I have just mentioned is one instance. And the case of the final "lie" to Marvin is in fact a more complex repetition than Sullivan suggests.

For the scene at the end of the book also looks back to an earlier scene with Marvin when he goes off to fight in the First World War. He comes to say goodbye to Hagar:

> I wanted all at once to hold him tightly, plead him with, against all reason and reality, not to go. But I did not want to embarrass both of us, nor have him think I'd taken leave of my senses. While I was hesitating, he spoke first.
>
> "I guess I won't be seeing you for quite a while," he said. "Think you'll be all right, here?"
>
> "All right?" I was released from my dithering, and could be

practical once more. "Of course we'll be all right, Marvin — why shouldn't we be? Well, you take care, now, and be sure to write. You'd better be getting along, or you'll not get into town in time to catch the train."

"Mother — "

"Yes?" And then I realized I was waiting with a kind of anxious hope for what he would say, waiting for him to make himself known to me.

But he never was a quick thinker, Marvin. Words would not come to his bidding, and so the moment eluded us both. He turned and put his hand on the door knob.

"Well, so long," he said. "I'll be seeing you." (124–30)

In the final scene they do speak, both of them, and the lie unties the knot between them, so that we feel, at the moment it is spoken, that it is suddenly metamorphosed into a truth:

"If I've been crabby with you, sometimes, these past years," he says in a low voice, "I didn't mean it."

I stare at him. Then, quite unexpectedly, he reaches for my hand and holds it tightly.

Now it seems to me he's truly Jacob, gripping with all his strength, and bargaining, *I will not let thee go, except thou bless me.* And I see I am thus strangely cast, and perhaps have been so from the beginning, and can only release myself by releasing him.

It's in my mind to ask his pardon, but that's not what he wants from me.

"You've not been cranky, Marvin. You've been good to me, always. A better son than John."

The dead don't bear a grudge nor seek a blessing. The dead don't rest uneasy. Only the living. Marvin, looking at me from anxious elderly eyes, believes me. It doesn't occur to him that a person in my place would ever lie.

"You got everything you want, here?" he says gruffly. "Anything you want me to bring you?"

"No, nothing, thanks."

"Well, so long," Marvin says. "I'll be seeing you." (304)

It is then, after giving the same farewell as when he went to the wars, that Marvin goes out and talks of his mother with anger and tenderness, saying: "[s]he's a holy terror" (304). That is the last she sees of him, as time hurries her to the end.

Time, as they say in contracts, is of the essence, and in Margaret Laurence's novels, time controls their structure and provides one of their recurrent themes.

A CLUSTER OF THEMES

Form in a work of literature is what most detaches it from life by imposing an aesthetic order on the chaos of existence. That is why the most formal art, which cuts all links with the world of appearance, is called abstract; it abstracts pure form from the world of visual complexities in which we live. But because it uses words, which have concrete meanings in everyday life, a work of literature can never be completely abstract. Theme is what sustains its link with living, by giving it a topic or idea that extends it beyond the aesthetic, and unites it with the preoccupations of humanity.

A work can have one theme or many, and Margaret Laurence's essential humanism makes it inevitable that in this respect her works are multifaceted. Her broad interest in the doings and the destiny of mankind, so strikingly exhibited early on in *The Prophet's Camel Bell*, was sufficient guarantee of that. But though she was a woman of strong and even passionate convictions — particularly on matters of war and peace, and racial discrimination — as a novelist she was essentially an organic writer. By this I mean that her themes tended to grow out of her characters and their situations rather than being imposed beforehand, and so we never get the idea that Laurence is setting out to teach us a political or a social lesson. What she does is to present us imaginatively with a specific instance of the human condition, the life of a person whose character determines her relationships with others and so to a great extent will determine her destiny. It is as this specific instance of human existence works itself out that we begin to generalize and say, in the case of *The Stone Angel*: "how typical of old women!" and then develop some broad

59

idea or theme to fit the case. Themes, of course, are really generalizations given fictional form.

Margaret Laurence is quite emphatic about the primacy of character in her novels; explaining the way they developed, she also isolates what she thought was the leading theme of *The Stone Angel*.

The individual characters come first, and I have often been halfway through something before I realized what the theme was. *The Stone Angel* fooled me even when I had finished writing it, for I imagined the theme was probably the same as in much of my African writing — the nature of freedom. This is partly true, but I see now that the emphasis by that time had altered. The world had changed; I had grown older. Perhaps I no longer believed so much in the promised land, even the promised land of one's own inner freedom. Perhaps an obsession with freedom is the persistent (thank God) dance of the young. With *The Stone Angel*, without my recognizing it at the time, the theme had changed to that of survival, the attempt of the personality to survive with some dignity, toting the load of excess mental baggage that everyone carries, until the moment of death. ("Ten Years' Sentences" 32)

Three years after Laurence wrote this essay, Margaret Atwood's *Survival* appeared (1972), picking survival as the central theme of Canadian writing. Surprisingly, the book contains only three quite brief references to *The Stone Angel*, and here it is evident that, while Atwood does not seem to think much of the book as a novel of survival, she does take up Laurence's first, abandoned position, and sees it as a novel about liberation, about frustrated attempts at liberation in a generational context:

Margaret Laurence's *The Stone Angel* has some model Grandparents. Hagar Shipley's stern father is a perfect Grandfather figure, and Hagar tries to rebel against him by marrying a source of earth energy, the disreputable but attractive farmer Bram. But she has soaked up too many of her father's principles, and she stifles Bram with her disapproval of him; instead of achieving liberation she has turned into a grandparent herself. Of her two sons, one takes the path of Parents and goes to the city, where he turns brownish-grey. The other tries to be a Child, in search of liberation, but there's not much scope for him; and when Hagar discovers his love affair and tortures him with her disapproval and moral rigidity, he gets himself killed in an accident. (136)

Atwood shows Hagar at the end of her life, with her anger returning, aiming "for a state in which acts which are 'truly free' will be possible."

> She does manage two free acts, and their seeming insignificance disappears when they are measured against the enormous weight of the imprisoning traditions she is struggling against. (143)

And she quotes Hagar's near-to-final thought, which appears on the penultimate page of the novel:

> I lie here and try to recall something truly free I've done in ninety years. I can think of only two acts that might be so, both recent. One was a joke — yet a joke only as all victories are, the paraphernalia being unequal to the event's reach. The other was a lie — yet not a lie, for it was spoken at least and at last with what may perhaps be a kind of love. (307)

I find Atwood's point convincing, and so I think we may assume that Laurence was right to begin with, and again at the end, and that the novel is about freedom *and* about survival. Hagar's long life is an often failing effort to find and be herself, and in that sense to achieve liberation, while survival itself is a kind of conditional and limited liberation from the prime necessity of human existence, which is death.

The theme of freedom takes us to another of the themes of *The Stone Angel*, one greatly expanded in Laurence's later novels. This is the theme of hostility between settlers and hunters, which has marred the whole history of North America. The contrast between Bram Shipley and Jason Currie which appeals to Hagar is that between the rigidities of the invading mercantilism represented by her father, a sanctimoniously Presbyterian self-made man, and the vanishing liberties of the frontier represented by Bram Shipley. "I thought he looked a bearded Indian, so brown and beaked a face" (45), she says, describing her first encounter with Bram. But in that slight remark is included all the ambivalence of her relationship with him, for it is precisely what she would regard as his "Indian" qualities — his lack of a Calvinist sense of propriety, his preference for horse breeding over farming, his predilection for the company of "half-breeds" — that she quickly comes to detest.

In the background of *The Stone Angel*, and challenging all the values of the Curries and of Manawaka, lives the half-breed clan of the Tonnerres, who figure in all of the Manawaka books (except *A Jest of God*, where their role of outsiders is assumed by the Ukrainian Kaslik family). They look on the town and its ways with laconic but contemptuous detachment, and they challenge the mores of its inhabitants with their independence from cares and conventions. Hagar's brother Matt and her son John both become involved with the Tonnerres, to neither's benefit, so that for Hagar the Métis boys appear not only as challengers but also as tempters.

> "I wouldn't have trusted any of them as far as I could spit. They lived all in a swarm in a shack somewhere — John always said their house was passably clean, but I gravely doubted it." (127)

Some of the important themes of *The Stone Angel* are inextricably entangled with other aspects of the novel which I have already been discussing. The nature of time and the role of memory in our lives — examined in the section entitled "An Architecture of Time" — is one of them, which has taken its place in my treatment of the novel's structure. Pride, discussed in the section "Character and Realism," is another. But linked with the matter of pride, which is a factor in Hagar's isolation, is the matter of personal relations. Why is it, Hagar is always asking, that she never seems really to know those who are close to her, though she may get on well with strangers? One of the most telling passages in the book is that in which John turns to her at a time when she is disappointed with his actions, and says: "You've always bet on the wrong horse. . . . Marv was your boy, but you never saw that, did you?" (237). In the end, of course, she does see it and grudgingly admits it, but it takes her a lifetime to do so. She is vaguely aware of that flaw in her perception:

> Right from the start, I either like a person or I don't. The only people I've ever been uncertain about were those closest to me. Maybe one looks at them too much. Strangers are easier to assess. (102)

As W.H. New has remarked in a cogent analysis of this aspect of Hagar's predicament, the problem of knowing others is, so far as she is concerned, closely linked with the problem of knowing herself.

> "How can one person know another?" Hagar is constantly asking; but "How can a person know himself?" is the deeper question that Margaret Laurence asks by implication. Even the first of these questions is double-edged. Hagar is not really known by the people around her nor can Hagar really know them. Only late in her life, when she sees more clearly her relationship with her sons — the favourite, flamboyant John; and the solidly middle-class Marvin with whom she lives — does she come really to see her very self, and hence to see and know her role in life. Only then can she accept for even a moment, for the sake of others, a role that is out of character for her, and discover in it some degree of that capacity for love which she has always craved and which she has always but unknowingly possessed. (Introduction, *The Stone Angel* vii)

This brings us back to the old Delphic command, "know thyself," which is the beginning of the knowledge of others. But the interesting thing, given Hagar's confession of greater ease with strangers, is that it is not her kin or her friends who play the most crucial and symbolically significant roles in the process of her self-recognition, and hence her liberation. Murray F. Lees, the preacher-turned insurance agent who guzzles cheap wine with her for a couple of midnight hours in the fish cannery, and the Reverend Troy, whom she meets on a couple of brief, embarrassed occasions, lead her farther on the road to liberation than either her friends, who have all died or disappeared by now; or Doris, who just wants to get her out of the house; or Marvin, who wants her blessing and has nothing more than his dull and dogged loyalty to offer in return. One is reminded that one of Margaret Laurence's most personal books was titled *Heart of a Stranger*. In it she says:

> I have spent a good many years of my adult life as a stranger in strange lands, in some cases as a resident, and in others as a traveller. I have met suspicion and mistrust at times, and I have also met with warmth and generosity. . . . One thing I learned, however, was that my experience of other countries probably

taught me more about myself and even my own land than it did about anything else. (11)

In the same way Hagar's encounters with strangers in the strange lands of the fish cannery and the hospital enlighten her mostly about herself. And so we should perhaps add the stranger in a strange land as a further theme of *The Stone Angel*.

Finally, there is the theme of old age leading to death, as distinct from that of survival. For *The Stone Angel* not only implicitly praises those who refuse to "go gentle into that good night," it also tells us that, however we may rage, the light will dim and we must be prepared for the unknown darkness. Life has been precious even if it has been filled with disappointment, even if its shortness takes one at ninety with a touch of surprise. At the same time, to face the unknown can be an adventure, and perhaps the greatest adventure of a long life. At her own insistence Hagar is taken out of the common ward at the hospital. But by the time it is all arranged, she has made friends with her wardmates and rather resents being taken from them and put into a semiprivate in comparative solitude.

> The world is even smaller now. It is shrinking so quickly. The next room will be the smallest of all.
> "The next room will be the smallest of the lot."
> "What?" the nurse says absent-mindedly, plumping my pillow.
> "Just enough space for me."
> She looks shocked. "That's no way to talk."
> How right she is. An embarrassing subject, better not mentioned. The way we used to feel, when I was a girl, about undergarments or the two-backed beast of love. But I want to take hold of her arm, force her attention. *Listen. You must listen. It's important. It's — quite an event.*
> Only to me. Not to her. I don't touch her arm, nor speak. It would only upset her. She wouldn't know what to say. (282)

Hagar has learnt at last to live with her own mortality, and that is the triumph of old age, the only triumph that, in life, we can have over death.

ORIGINALITY AND ORIGINS

To try and trace the literary sources of a truly original writer often seems a hard and pedantic task. True, there are some critics and cultural historians who assure us that all literature is derived from other literature, since the forms are constant. We can perhaps accept the argument in the same way as we can accept the argument that all speech is derived from a common pool of language, and is more or less in accord with common rules that were established when the languages were frozen by the Académie française and Johnson's dictionary and similar moves toward uniformity. But we are still left with the fact that within given literatures and languages people express themselves in utterly different ways and that, though they may accept certain conventions of form — as Margaret Laurence accepts with modifications the form of the realist novel as developed by Gustave Flaubert, Henry James, Ivan Turgenev, and others in the nineteenth century — it is more difficult to isolate specific influences. Derivative writers reveal their derivations; original writers conceal theirs and that is part of their originality. But it does not mean that they are lacking in masters or models.

In the case of Margaret Laurence we have to remember that Neepawa, her native town, influenced her in several ways. It offered a microcosm of western Canadian life which she appropriated and adapted to her own use. It also offered the speech patterns of her parents and grandparents, which she freely and frequently admitted to using in her novels. And finally, it offered at least two important sources of early literary influence.

One of these was the United Church, which she attended as a child and to which she adhered, at least nominally, all her life. For many years she attended its services, and though the hymns she must have sung do not play the same role in her books as they do in Marian Engel's novel of the religious life, *The Glassy Sea* (1978), the Bible — in the grandly eloquent King James Version which lies at the roots of English prose — is abundantly present. Its phrases ring through the prose of Hagar's narrative, and its desert images recur throughout *The Stone Angel*. Though the New Testament has its turn in Laurence's later books, the Old Testament is dominant in *The Stone Angel* — the Old Testament that reflected the stern attitudes of her own Scots Presbyterian ancestors. Indeed, one often has the sense that the characters are driven by the Jehovah who called himself "a jealous God."

Nevertheless, when she comes to using the book of Genesis as a model for her novel, Margaret Laurence plays fast and loose with it. Hagar may be a wanderer like her namesake, but it is her father Jason rather than her husband Bram who presumes to the patriarchal role of Abraham, though fate frustrates him as his two sons die childless. One first assumes that Hagar's son John is cast in the role of Ishmael; his defiance of convention and his association with the seminomadic Tonnerres might seem to confirm this conclusion. But then one finds a biblical generation skipped, John and Marvin share the role of Jacob, as John wrestles with the angel in the cemetery, trying to set it erect again, and Marvin becomes "truly Jacob" at Hagar's end, and silently bargains: *"I will not let thee go, except thou bless me"* (304).

In her own way, Laurence treats her biblical sources as cavalierly as Timothy Findley treats the story of Noah in *Not Wanted on the Voyage*. Like many modern writers, she takes the attitude that the demands of the imagination leave no material sacred or immune from transformation. We can therefore expect her to be no less independent in her attitude to the writers who may have in some way influenced her than she is to the Bible; it is impossible to think of her as any other writer's disciple. Yet she read widely and profited from her reading.

The second source of literary influence in Neepawa was the local library, which was run by Margaret Wemyss's stepmother, who chose her books well and encouraged her stepdaughter to read them. Clearly, from childhood onward, Laurence's reading was wide. The references in her writings and her interviews show the influence of an eclectic range of books, mainly in the English tradition; she is liable to bring in references ranging anywhere from Shakespeare to Joyce (though her tastes do not appear to be especially daring). Among non-Canadian writers, she seems most at home with writers who fit into the same broad field of realism as she: writers like Graham Greene, E.M. Forster, and especially Joyce Cary, of whom I will say more later.

To talk of reading is one thing; to talk of identifiable influence is another. Laurence clearly learnt her literary language through the great readings of her childhood and youth; she did not have the opportunity to take part in a creative writing school and was certainly the better for having escaped such a pseudo-àcademic approach to literature. She developed within the ambience of the literature of her time, and the goals she acquired were the general ones of mid-twentieth-century fiction: the development of character, the exploration of time and memory. Though she was not entirely an unpolitical person, and in her sympathies stood on the moderate Left, she was an unpolitical writer in the sense that she did not see literature as having a didactic purpose, and anything like the ideologically charged writing of the socialist realists of Russia and their Western imitators would have been anathema to her.

Thus it is fairly easy to place Laurence within a literary context, but more easy to find analogies and resemblances than influences. This I think is largely because of the special experience which Laurence herself felt differentiated her as a writer. She started to write in Africa, where the problem of coping with a strange culture monopolized her attention. She remained isolated from the Canadian literary scene — except for her college friendship with Adele Wiseman — until her return to Vancouver in 1957 in her early thirties, when she slowly found her way into the Canadian literary world. It was, I suspect, largely this isolation in a series of strange cultures — Moslem and then animist — that enabled her to strike out so much on her own when she came home. Indeed, the publication of *The Stone Angel* was hailed as marking the appearance of a new and original literary talent on the Canadian literary horizon, and rapidly made Laurence the most important novelist in that vitally formative period of Canadian writing — the late 1960s and early 1970s.

So let us seek analogies and parallels rather than influences. S.E. Read once remarked that Hagar Shipley was a "Lear-like figure" (41), and here we can perhaps think in terms of the adoption of an archetype first strikingly developed by Shakespeare rather than of the borrowing of a character. True, Hagar, like Lear, gives up her worldly goods into the hands of her child, and is shocked and angered to discover how this act has destroyed her freedom. True, also, her flight to the cannery may be regarded as parallel to Lear's flight to the blasted heath. One might, with no great stretch of the imagination, equate Murray F. Lees with the fool and see Doris as a weak version of Goneril-Regan. But where is Cordelia? And where does Marvin fit in? In any case, the heart of the novel does not lie all in the present, to which its echoes of the Lear myth are restricted, but largely in Hagar's past, which is different from anything in *King Lear*.

We experience similar difficulties if we look to Canadian literature for specific influences. Laurence herself was very conscious of her position within a developing tradition. She always spoke of Canadian writers as a tribe, and stressed the importance of those one might call its elders as an example. In 1983 she said to Rosemary Sullivan:

> The generation of writers older than myself — and I have said this quite often — have meant a great deal to all of us. Sinclair Ross, Hugh MacLennan, Morley Callaghan, Gabrielle Roy, Ernest Buckler, Ethel Wilson, and so on — all these writers, a lot of them lived in considerable isolation from each other, and actually, they were really the pioneering generation. They were the first generation of Canadian novelists to write out their own people and their own culture, the sight of their own eyes, not taking as their models British or American writers, but developing the consciousness of their own people and culture. And I have always said, and I profoundly believe — I say it to young writers all the time — we all of us owe them a great deal. (78–79)

What distinguishes the writers she lists, when we think of their work, is how different they were from each other, except in the sense that they broke away from alien models and saw their land and their culture with their own eyes. Their very isolation helped to create that individuality, and in the same way Laurence's early isolation in Africa and then in Vancouver is part of the explanation of why she was so strikingly fresh and original when she published *The Stone Angel*.

Of the writers she mentioned she is probably closest to Sinclair Ross and Ethel Wilson. Ethel Wilson, who admired her early African stories and wrote to her about them, became her friend, and one can see the affinities that brought them together. Both wrote mostly through women's perceptions and about women, and they shared that feeling for place which comes out so strongly in Wilson's novels about British Columbia and in Laurence's evocation of the Manitoba prairie and the environs of Vancouver. Self-liberation and old age also concerned them both. But there is not a great deal in common between Wilson's old woman character, the gentle egotist Topaz in *The Innocent Traveller* (1949), and proud abrasive Hagar. And while

Maggie Vardoe in Wilson's *Swamp Angel* (1954) flees from her marriage in middle age as Hagar does, she goes into liberation and fulfilment, while Hagar carries with her the enslaving burden of her pride.

Laurence's relationship with Sinclair Ross is closer. As she told Robert Kroetsch:

> I remember — I must have been in my late teens, I suppose — when I read Sinclair Ross's novel, *As for Me and My House*, which was about a minister in a small prairie town; it hit me with tremendous force, because I realized for the first time that people could really write about my background. (154)

In that sense, *As for Me and My House* was an influence which turned Margaret Laurence toward writing about the prairies. Her interest in Ross's work was so far maintained that she wrote the introduction to his volume of stories, *The Lamp at Noon* (1968). But apart from the fact that their books share a prairie small-town setting and biblical echoes (fainter in Ross than in Laurence), they do not have enough in common to propose *As for Me and My House* as a model for *The Stone Angel*.

The one writer who may really have influenced Margaret Laurence was the English novelist Joyce Cary. Their careers were strikingly similar. Joyce Cary spent some years in Africa, four decades before Laurence was there, and wrote his first books about the continent and its people. Then he turned to his own country and wrote a remarkable series of novels about the English, of which *The Horse's Mouth* (1944) is the best known. Clara Thomas wrote on the relationship between the two writers in an essay entitled "Pilgrim's Progress: Margaret Laurence and Hagar Shipley." She claims that Laurence discovered Cary's novels when she returned from Africa to Vancouver: "When in 1969 I first asked her about other novelists' influence on her work, his was the only name she gave me; she has recently confirmed this once again" (163).

The books by Cary that most influenced Laurence are the group he wrote in the 1940s: *Herself Surprised* (1941), *To Be a Pilgrim* (1942), and *The Horse's Mouth* (1944). In each of them a character tells the story in which they are all involved from his or her point of view. The novel nearest *The Stone Angel* is *Herself Surprised*, in which an old woman, Sara Monday, reveals her long and raffish life.

Both Sara and Hagar are survivors, but the novels differ greatly in tone, since Hagar's life is dominated by the rigours of her Calvinist upbringing whereas Sara is a guilt-free sensualist. As Thomas puts it: "Sara's story . . . moves in light compared with the blackness that encircles Hagar" ("Pilgrim's Progress" 166). What must have struck Laurence most of all — and what remains as a palpable presence in *The Stone Angel* — was the complexity and subtlety of Cary's first person narration, and in this she proved an adept pupil of her only master.

MADAME BOVARY . . . ?

Having reached the conclusion that Margaret Laurence's vision is entirely original and her methods almost so, we come back to that obstinate issue: the relationship between the author and the character she created. For *The Stone Angel* in an important way *is* Hagar — all the other characters fall away into comparative insignificance, while her presence haunts our memory.

Margaret Laurence resolutely denied that Hagar was a mask for herself, and she described her kind of novel as "one in which the fictional characters are very definitely *themselves*, not me, the kind of novel in which I can feel a deep sense of connection with the main character without a total identification which for me would prevent a necessary distancing" ("A Place" 16).

But in what does the "deep sense of connection" exist if not in identification? I would suggest it is one of speech, and that in speech lies the problem that has haunted many readers and which gave Margaret Laurence herself at least some moments of anxiety. In her essay "Gadgetry or Growing," she tells us that:

> Another problem I encountered in *The Stone Angel* was the question of how far a woman such as Hagar would have thoughts in which places and events are described partly in terms of poetic imagery. Were the descriptions of the forest, for example, or the prairie in the drought — all the descriptions which

came naturally as I was writing the book — were these in fact Hagar or were they me? I worried about this quite a lot, because I did not want Hagar to think out of character, and I recognize this as one difficulty of first-person narration — the lack of external viewpoint, in fact the abolishing of the narrator. On the other hand, I could not really believe those descriptions *were* out of character. I don't know why I felt this, but I simply felt they were right when I was actually doing them. They seemed like Hagar. Truthfully, I did not even think about this whole question when I was writing the novel. It was only afterwards, in the rewriting, that I worried. I finally came to the conclusion that even people who are relatively inarticulate, in their relationships with other people, are perfectly capable within themselves of perceiving the world in more poetic terms (although I mistrust that expression) than their outer voices might indicate. (83–84)

This matter of inner and outer voices raises the point that in an important way *The Stone Angel* is *about* speech, although speech is not an actual theme. Margaret Laurence tells us how, at the beginning, the speech patterns and the characters seemed to come together. "I kept feeling that I *knew* I was getting the speech exactly right. It was *mine*" (Sullivan 68). I think we can take that use of "mine" in two ways: it is, as she later explains, the speech of her grandparents and her parents; but it is hers too, as well as Hagar's.

One of the things that strikes one about Hagar is not only that she speaks — inwardly of course — copiously and vividly, but also that she is aware of her own compulsion to speak, to explain, to record. Toward the end of the novel, when her grandson Steven comes to see her, she is angry with the fact that, though her thoughts flow freely, she is unable to communicate them to him, to get through.

I'm choked with it now, the incommunicable years, everything that happened and was spoken or not spoken. I want to tell him. Someone should know. This is what I think. *Someone really ought to know these things.* (296)

And, of course, we the readers do know them, for Hagar, in her own way, has "written" her tale like a book, and we accept or distrust her as much as we do any other author.

Here, I think, we come to the links between Laurence and her characters. She is fascinated with speech; she makes them speak, inwardly or outwardly, in their various ways, but in the process they become captivated by the words and the pictures they offer. In their restless inner monologues they reveal themselves to be unfulfilled authors, writers manqués, progressing through the novels until, in *The Diviners*, Morag Gunn is at last, like her creator, a writer who has found herself. She is no longer lost, as Hagar is, in the "incommunicable years."

Works Cited

Atwood, Margaret. *Survival: A Thematic Guide to Canadian Literature*. Toronto: Anansi, 1972.

Atwood does not see *The Stone Angel* as a novel of survival; it is a novel about liberation, particularly frustrated attempts at liberation in a generational context.

Callaghan, Barry. "The Writings of Margaret Laurence." *Tamarack Review* 36 (1965): 45–51.

A descriptive account of Laurence's work up to and including *The Stone Angel*.

Cameron, Donald. "Margaret Laurence: The Black Celt Speaks of Freedom." *Conversations with Canadian Novelists*. 2 vols. Vol. 1. Toronto: Macmillan, 1973. 96–115.

Davies, Robertson. "Self-Imprisoned to Keep the World at Bay." *New York Times Book Review* 14 June 1964: 4–5, 33.

Djwa, Sandra. "False Gods and the True Covenant: Thematic Continuity between Margaret Laurence and Sinclair Ross." *Journal of Canadian Fiction* 1.4 (1972): 43–50.

Fabre, Michel. "From *The Stone Angel* to *The Diviners*: An Interview with Margaret Laurence." Woodcock, *A Place to Stand On* 46–55.

Gibson, Graeme. *Eleven Canadian Novelists*. Toronto: Anansi, 1973.

Hind–Smith, Joan. *Three Voices: The Lives of Margaret Laurence, Gabrielle Roy, Frederick Philip Grove*. Toronto: Clarke, 1975.

Klinck, Carl F., ed. *Literary History of Canada*. 2nd ed. 3 vols. Toronto: U of Toronto P, 1976.

Laurence, Margaret. *A Bird in the House: Stories*. Toronto: McClelland, 1970.

———. *The Diviners*. Toronto: McClelland, 1974.

———. *The Fire-Dwellers*. Toronto: McClelland, 1969.

———. "Gadgetry or Growing: Form and Voice in the Novel." *A Place to Stand On: Essays by and about Margaret Laurence*. Ed. George Woodcock. Edmonton: NeWest, 1980. 80–92.

Examines the relationship between Laurence and the characters created by her.

———. *Heart of a Stranger*. Toronto: McClelland, 1976.

———. *A Jest of God*. Toronto: McClelland, 1966.

———. *Long Drums and Cannons: Nigerian Novelists and Dramatists*. London: Macmillan, 1968.

———. "A Place to Stand On." Woodcock, *A Place to Stand On* 15–19.

Discusses the reality of remembered experience behind Laurence's fictional community of Manawaka.

———. *The Prophet's Camel Bell.* Toronto: McClelland, 1963.

———. *The Stone Angel.* New Canadian Library 59. Toronto: McClelland, 1968.

———. "Ten Years' Sentences." Woodcock, *A Place to Stand On* 10–16.

Laurence discusses the conception and development of character in her novels.

———. *This Side Jordan.* Toronto: McClelland, 1960.

———. *The Tomorrow–Tamer.* New Canadian Library 70. Toronto: McClelland, 1970.

———. "Time and the Narrative Voice." Woodcock, *A Place to Stand On* 155–59.

Laurence examines the relationship between her kind of writer and the characters she creates, and discusses the treatment of time and the handling of narrative voice in her works.

———. *A Tree for Poverty: Somali Poetry and Prose.* Hamilton, ON: McMaster U Library P, 1970.

Morley, Patricia. *Margaret Laurence.* Twayne's World Authors Series 591. Boston: Twayne, 1981.

New, William H. "Every Now and Then: Voice and Language in Laurence's *The Stone Angel.*" Woodcock, *A Place to Stand On* 171–92.

———. Introduction. *The Stone Angel.* New Canadian Library 59. Toronto: McClelland, 1968. iii–x.

Includes an examination of one aspect of Hagar's predicament, that of personal identity. The problem of knowing others is closely linked with the problem of knowing oneself.

———. "Life and Time: Laurence's *The Stone Angel.*" New, *Articulating West* 207–15.

———, ed. *Margaret Laurence: The Writer and Her Critics.* Critical Views on Canadian Writers. Toronto: McGraw, 1977.

Read, S.E. "The Maze of Life: The Work of Margaret Laurence." Woodcock, *A Place to Stand On* 35–45.

A descriptive account of Laurence's work up to and including *The Stone Angel.* Read sees Hagar as a "Lear-like figure."

Renault, Mary. "On Understanding Africa." Rev. of *This Side Jordan. Saturday Review* Dec. 1960: 23–24.

Sullivan, Rosemary. "An Interview with Margaret Laurence." Woodcock, *A Place to Stand On* 61–79.

Thomas, Clara. *The Manawaka World of Margaret Laurence.* Toronto: McClelland, 1975.

———. *Margaret Laurence.* Canadian Writers Series 3. Toronto: McClelland, 1969.

———. "Pilgrim's Progress: Margaret Laurence and Hagar Shipley." Woodcock, *A Place to Stand On* 160–71.

Discusses the influence of Joyce Cary's novels on Laurence's work.

Tracy, Honour. "A Writer of Major Talent." *New Republic* 20 June 1964: 19–20.

Warwick, Susan. "Margaret Laurence: An Annotated Bibliography." *The Annotated Bibliography of Canada's Major Authors*. Ed. Robert Lecker and Jack David. Vol. 1. Toronto: ECW, 1979. 47–101.

Wiseman, Adele. "Somali Literature." *Queen's Quarterly* 62 (1956): 610–11.

Woodcock, George. "The Human Elements: Margaret Laurence's Fiction." *The Human Elements: Critical Essays*. Ed. David Helwig. Ottawa: Oberon, 1978. 134–61.

A study of the archetypal aspects of Laurence's novels, particularly *The Stone Angel*.

Woodcock, George. *A Place to Stand On: Essays by and about Margaret Laurence*. Western Canadian Literary Documents Series 4. Edmonton: NeWest, 1980.

_____. *The World of Canadian Writing: Critiques and Recollections*. Vancouver: Douglas, 1980.

Index